Effective
Communication

Nicholas Harvey

Gill & Macmillan

Gill & Macmillan Ltd
Hume Avenue
Park West
Dublin 12
with associated companies throughout the world
www.gillmacmillan.ie

© 2002 Nicholas Harvey
0 7171 3249 8
Print origination in Ireland by Graham Thew Design

*The paper used in this book is made from the
wood pulp of managed forests.
For every tree felled, at least one tree is planted,
thereby renewing natural resources.*

A catalogue record is available for this book from
the British Library.

Contents

Preface

Effective Communication was written in response to a demand for a course book for students studying for the FETAC Level 2 Communications Module. It is also suitable for students who are taking any course in communications or for those with a general interest in the subject.

It attempts to cover as wide a range of skills as possible within the confines of a college textbook. It is divided into seven parts.

Part 1: Introduction

Begins with a brief outline of communication as a particularly human trait and a look at the communication revolution occurring today with all its challenges and possibilities. It also examines why and how we communicate and introduces the reader to the basic process of communication. Perception and culture are at the very root of communication, and chapter 2 discusses topics such as prejudice, social communities, gender and intercultural communication, which have become vital issues in today's multicultural society.

Part 2: The Written Word

Deals with the basic skills of reading and writing and offers hints for improvement. It covers the different types of personal and functional writing needed for vocational and social situations, including samples of letters, memos, reports etc. There is also a chapter on how to research and produce an assignment for a course at college.

Part 3: Non-verbal Communication

Investigates the various ways we communicate without words such as body language, facial expression, sounds and visual signs. The chapter on visual communication explains how to interpret and produce images; an important new area considering much of the information we receive today comes to us through visual media.

Part 4: Interpersonal Communication

Offers the reader a look at some fundamentals on how we interact with other people. It suggests ways of creating a healthy communication environment between people, how to deal with conflict and how to improve assertiveness. It is useful preparation for the following section on speaking.

Part 5: The Spoken Word

Deals with speaking and listening skills and the various situations that demand them. There is emphasis on the use of the voice, dialogue and negotiation skills, interviews, group interaction, meetings and extensive preparation for the oral presentation.

Part 6: Communication Technology

Covers the telephone, computers, the Internet and email, their uses and influence on our lives today. Relevant skills include telephone technique, how to go online, search and make the most of the Internet, and how to use and how not to use email. The problems and pitfalls of the various technologies are also scrutinised. There are suggested websites for further research, and computer and Internet instructions apply to personal computers (PCs), being the most widely used type of computer.

Part 7: Mass Communication

Is a critical examination of the mass media, its influence in the world today, the various aspects of control and legislation that apply to it and some thoughts on media appreciation and production.

At the start of each chapter is a list of skills pertinent to FETAC assessment requirements as well as the topics to be covered in that chapter. Some chapters, which do not directly pertain to FETAC assessment, offer support information, preparation for assessments, and/or material for class discussion. Points for discussion and activities are included in each chapter to help put some of the most essential skills into practice. This is to encourage active participation by students, and provides opportunities for expressing views and for developing speaking skills.

Post Leaving Cert/Further Education attracts such a wide range of students of differing ages and abilities that tutors and class groups can decide for themselves how to proceed with discussions and activities in a way they feel is appropriate to their individual requirements e.g. division in smaller groups, pair work etc. Activities that are applicable to FETAC assessment are labelled 'Assessment Activities'.

The book need not be read or studied in the order in which it is presented. It is possible to select and dip into chapters that are found to be of particular interest or relevance.

Communication is not something we can become experts at in a year or two. It is a skill that can be refined over a lifetime and at the end we still won't have mastered it all. This book serves as an introduction to the main topics and themes. Oscar Wilde said, 'Nothing that is worth knowing can be taught'. Communication skills are best learnt by doing, by practising and by experiencing. So take the ideas in this book and try them out by putting them into practice yourself.

The personal pronouns 'he', 'she', 'him' and 'her' are used randomly throughout the book.

Acknowledgements

I would like to thank the following:

For their help with proof reading and suggestions: Jenny Alford, Frances Gaynor, Niina Hepojoki, George Jacob and especially Anne Geraghty, who made me feel like an inept student all over again, but who was tireless and thorough with her constructive criticism and enormous contribution.

For a vital telephone lesson in document layout, Marian Bryan.

For general support and encouragement, the staff and students at Sallynoggin College of Further Education.

For kind permission to reproduce her story, Angel, Maria Raha.

For kind permission to use his film review from *In Dublin*, reviewer, Garreth Murphy and editor, Tom Galvin.

For putting up with all my telephone calls and answering my questions, Ailbhe O'Reilly and Deirdre Greenan at Gill & Macmillan.

Nicholas Harvey

The Publishers are grateful to the following for permission to reproduce material used in the book:

Camera Press for pictures of faces with different expressions: the Beatles; Jackie Kennedy; Tattooed Man; Eye Contact; Citizen Traveller for Citizen Traveller poster; Rudi Miel for Cartoon of Chain Racism; Randy Glasbergen for Cartoon 'If we eliminate vowels and punctuation from all corporate communications, we can save €400 a year on ink and toner'; *The Irish Times* and Frank Miller for photo of two women (Bodily Contact); *The Irish Times* and Cyril Byrne for photo of Berti Ahern and Romano Prodi; *The Irish Times* and Cyril Byrne for photo of Republican Militiaman; Photocall for pictures of Brian Cowen, Síle de Valera and Brian Farrell; Associated Press for photo of Kim Phuc and Climate Accident; Fantagraphic Books Inc, Seattle for cartoon by Mark Kalesnicko; Popperfoto for demonstration photos of G8 Summit in Genoa; Faber and Faber for 'Digging' from *Death of a Naturalist* by Seamus Heaney; Tom Mathews and *The Irish Times* for his cartoon; Kathryn Holmquist for 'More to Male Bonding than Beer and Football', *The Irish Times*; Allsorts Media for cartoons of Hagar the Horrible.

While every care has been taken to trace and acknowledge copyright the Publishers tender their apologies for any accidental infringement where copyright has proved untraceable. They would be pleased to come to a suitable arrangement with the rightful owner in each case.

Part 1
Introduction

Chapter 1 Introduction to Communication

 To Communicate is Human

Between 100,000 and 30,000 years ago two species of human, Homo sapiens (modern humans) and Neanderthals, lived side by side in parts of Europe and the Middle East. According to fossil records, the Neanderthals died out around 30,000 years ago and Homo sapiens survived. Anthropologists believe that one of the reasons we survived was because of unique communication skills.

Humans are physically better equipped to communicate than most other species. We have a large brain, which can process and produce complicated language, and a tongue, jaw and throat, which are shaped to produce a wider variety of sounds than other animals. We also have the urge to make contact with others. We are a social species. These abilities helped early Homo sapiens because important and detailed information about survival would have been shared with others, while the ill-equipped Neanderthals, keeping to themselves in small isolated groups eventually became extinct.

Fast forward to the twenty first century and we are being bombarded by huge amounts of information, which are communicated via a vast array of technologies from all over the world. The Communications Revolution has created an entirely new range of communication tools: the Internet, mobile phones, digital television, email etc. These are all changing the ways we communicate with one another and in turn we need to learn new skills to master them.

Just as communication helped our species survive in the past, it seems it can still help us survive today's fast paced technology driven world. Information is a key to this survival. In order to have access to the latest information, be it about health, education, business, shopping, entertainment, or just social contact with others, we need to be able to communicate to find it and exchange it.

However, for all the marvels of technology that enable us to speak instantly to someone thousands of miles away, we are often still at a loss as to how to actually express ourselves. When it comes down to actually saying to someone what we want to say we find we often come unstuck. Words we use amongst our close friends won't necessarily impress a potential employer. We can't use words like 'cool' or 'crap' in an interview or a formal letter of complaint because we won't be taken seriously. The abbreviated language we use in emails and text messages are fine for informal situations, but we can't write 'I cn a10d an ntrvu @ ne time,' in a letter of application!

In order to survive in the Information Age we need to be adaptable, flexible and to have at our disposal a wide range of communication skills. We can use the technologies available to us but we also need the skills to know what to say, how to say it and when it is appropriate to say it. The more ways we can communicate, the better equipped we are to deal with the modern world.

Communication and language are uniquely human traits. In a sense, learning how to communicate is about becoming more human. Some people have a natural flair for it and others don't. But no matter how good or bad we think we are as communicators, all communication skills can be learned and improved upon.

What Is Communication?

The word 'communication' comes from the Latin word *communicare*, which means to share, impart or make common. How well we communicate is often determined by how easily we can share or impart information or find common ground with other people.

Communication is an active process that is forever changing. Language doesn't stay the same. It evolves and we don't use the same English today that Shakespeare did. Almost every time we speak we somehow put together a collection of words that we have never used before. When two people are put together, eventually they are going to start communicating with each other, and neither has any idea where they will end up. A frightening thought, perhaps, but an exciting one as well. However, we can do a certain amount of planning and preparation for specific communication scenarios to prevent communication breaking down.

We can define communication as an exchange of messages between two people or two groups of people.

Why Do We Communicate?

In their book *More than Words*, Richard Dimbleby and Graeme Burton list twelve needs and purposes of communication.

Survival

We need to communicate to buy food and clothing; rent or buy accommodation; seek help from others if we are sick or in danger, all of which are necessary for survival.

Co-operation

We communicate for the purpose of trade; to exchange ideas and information; for the enjoyment of interaction or just to get on with other people.

Personal Needs

As humans we have a basic need for contact with others. Exchanging thoughts and feelings can help satisfy our personal needs.

Relationships

Relationships are formed and sustained by communication. Problems that occur within relationships are often a result of a lack of communication. One of the best ways to sort out problems is by talking about them.

Persuasion

In our everyday communication with others we may use persuasion more than we think. Whether we are trying to convince potential employers that we are the best person for the job, persuading a college tutor to give us a deadline extension or trying to borrow money we are using persuasion to get what we want.

Power

We communicate for power by winning arguments and by impressing others with our knowledge and skill as communicators. More negatively, we can misuse it by making others feel inferior by putting them down.

Societal Needs

Communication within and between all the different organisations in our society is crucial for it to function properly. Government departments, schools, colleges, hospitals and businesses would collapse without proper communication facilities to help run them.

Economic

Buying and selling cannot take place without some form of communication between the buyer and the seller. Advertising also plays a role in this process.

Information

Information is fundamental to human existence. It may be something as simple as reading a sell by date on a food item or being told the time. Gossip is information, although it may not always be accurate! We send emails and letters to let friends and relatives know how we are and what we're doing. The media inform us about people and events in the world and advertising informs us about products. What we learn at school and college, education, is all information.

Making Sense of the World

Children are naturally inquisitive. They often ask questions beginning with 'Why?' in order to make sense of the world around them. As adults we also ask similar questions when we need to understand something and to give events and situations meaning.

Decision-making

When a couple talk about what to do on a date they are making a decision. When a company holds a board meeting to discuss the potential of a new product it is making decisions.

Self-expression

When we are involved in the creative process, we communicate by tapping into the imagination and expressing ourselves in an artistic way:
1. Visual – painting, drawing, sculpture etc.
2. Writing – poetry, stories, etc.
3. Music
4. Dance
5. Body adornment – make-up, jewellery, etc.
6. Drama.

How Do We Communicate?

Every time some form of communication occurs, there is a specific process that takes place. We can break this process down into its different parts so that we can see what exactly is happening. By looking at how we communicate, we can become better communicators. Keywords are in italics.

Basically a *sender* (a person or group of people) conceives a message and sends it (information, thought, feeling etc.) to a *receiver* (another person or group of people).

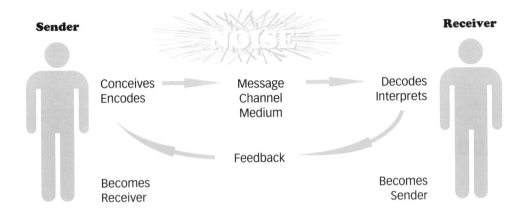

Fig. 1.1. Diagram of model of communication process.

The message is encoded, *code* being the language used by the sender. It may refer to the actual language that we speak, e.g. English, Irish etc. or it can refer to verbal, e.g. spoken and written language, or non-verbal, e.g. body-language, facial expression, signals etc.

The *message* is transmitted by a *medium*, e.g. phone call, email, letter etc. and travels along a *channel*, e.g. telephone line, postal system etc.

The *receiver* receives the message and decodes it, i.e. makes sense of it. Some messages are literal. Others can contain implied meanings that may be misinterpreted. The receiver, then, also has to *interpret* the message for other meanings. 'Do you want to come back to my place for coffee?' literally means an offer of coffee. What is its implied meaning?

Feedback is given. This is when the receiver sends another message back to the sender to reply or to acknowledge receipt of the first message.

Once feedback has been given, the process continues with another message from sender to receiver and so on.

Fig. 1.2 The language code!

Noise is any kind of interference that interferes with or prevents the successful transmission of the message. It can be:

- Physical – roadworks outside a building interrupting a conversation
- Emotional – mistrust between the sender and receiver may interfere with the message
- Psychological – a receiver who is tired will find it difficult to take in a lengthy complicated message
- Technological – fear of computers often prevents some people using them to communicate.

The *context* is the situation in which the communication takes place. It usually refers to the time and place, but may also include the people involved. The context can influence the way we communicate. In a work context, communication is likely to be more formal than it would be in a nightclub.

Activity

1. One-way communication

Divide into groups of four or five. One person in each group will be the sender of a message and the rest will be the receivers. The sender chooses one of the shapes in appendix 1 of the book and tries to describe it using words only. The receivers, who are not allowed to speak, will try to draw the shape from the sender's description.

2. Two-way communication

Remain in the same groups and do the same activity as above, except this time, the receivers may speak, and ask any questions they might have.

The purpose of this activity is to illustrate that in order for communication to be effective it has to be a two-way process. In the first activity (one-way), there was incomplete communicating going on as no feedback was permitted. The two-way communication probably took longer, but the message will have been more accurate. Discuss any problems and difficulties experienced by both senders and receivers during this activity. One common mistake we make is to assume the receiver has more knowledge than he actually does.

The Media of Communication

We can put all types of communication into five media groups:

1. Written
2. Oral
3. Visual
4. Technological
5. Mass Media.

Discussion

Briefly discuss a few examples for each medium. Some examples may belong to more than one group. Television, for example, can make use of all five, but might best belong to Mass Media. What are the advantages and disadvantages of each medium?

Media Appropriateness

Some of the worst mistakes in communication are as a result of using an inappropriate medium. There is no point in a company informing all its shareholders about a new business venture by telephone. It would be too time consuming. A famous film star once finished his relationship with his girlfriend by sending her a fax. Is this an appropriate medium for this type of communication?

Activity

What media of communication would you choose for the following and why:

1. Applying for a job
2. Firing someone from a job
3. Complaining about a holiday to a travel agent
4. Offering sympathy to the family (living abroad) of a friend who has died
5. Explaining a personal problem to your boss
6. Requesting information about different types of bank account
7. Informing customers to switch off mobile phones as they enter the cinema
8. Advertising a new leisure complex in a hotel
9. Asking for a bank loan
10. Informing a colleague that you resent his/her offensive behaviour
11. Telling the board of directors of a company your new marketing strategy
12. Informing your class tutor that you are sick on the day of an assignment deadline
13. Advertising a concert you've organised in your local community hall
14. Letting colleagues (10 or more) know about a meeting to be held the next day
15. Sending a list of costs and rates of the hotel you work in to a potential customer arriving in Ireland from Italy in two days
16. Asking someone on a date
17. Seeking a quote for paper and ink for your printers
18. A tutor giving students important information about an assignment – a brief, number of words required, deadline etc.
19. Complaining to a neighbour about persistent noise late at night
20. An electrician supplying a quote for a job he's been asked to do
21. Letting students in college know about the Christmas Social
22. Resigning from your job
23. Informing a client that their payment for goods received is overdue

A Guide to Effective Communication

Here are some tips for improving our general communication skills and awareness.

As Sender

Conceive the message carefully

Decide what your communication objectives are. Do you want to inform, entertain, impress, persuade or get information? Aim for clarity and avoid vagueness, ambiguity and unnecessary jargon.

Have Empathy

This means understanding where the receiver is coming from, her beliefs, feelings, values and interests. Put yourself in the receiver's shoes. She may not see things the way you do.

Choose an Appropriate Code and Medium

Choose a code that the receiver understands and a tone that is appropriate. We wouldn't use the same tone talking to our employer as we would to a child. Choose an appropriate medium.

Consider the Context (Time and Place)

Attempting to communicate with someone who is too busy to listen to us will inevitably fail. Reprimanding someone for a misdemeanour should take place somewhere private and not in a public place in front of others.

Check for Feedback

As a sender it is vital to know that the message has been received and understood. Ask if it's okay.

As Receiver

Pay attention

Many messages are lost due to lack of concentration.

Decode Correctly

Make sure you understand the message and if not, seek clarification. Be aware of implied meanings in messages.

Give Feedback

Always let the sender know you've received and understood the message. A simple nod or 'Yes' is often enough to show the sender you've got the message. Without feedback, the sender is left unsure about the message. Was it sent? Was it understood? If a message is unclear the receiver should seek clarification, giving feedback to say so.

Activities

List five examples of communication you took part in during the past twenty-four hours. In each case state the following:
1. The purpose of each communication
2. If you were the sender or receiver
3. If the message was well conceived
4. The choice of code, medium and channel
5. The context in which each took place
6. The feedback given
7. Whether there was any noise
8. Whether each communication was successful
9. Whether there was room for improvement.

Chapter Review

1. What makes communication a uniquely human experience?
2. What are the chief purposes of communication?
3. Outline the main stages in the communication process.
4. Explain the importance of feedback.
5. Why is it important to choose the appropriate medium for communication?
6. Explain the following:
   • Code   • Channel   • Noise   • Context.

Points for Discussion

1. When do we not communicate?
2. Are we better or worse communicators than our parents?
3. One of the biggest communication problems is that we don't communicate enough.
4. Discuss how a lack of communication might be harmful to the following:
   • Personal relationships/marriages
   • Amongst employees
   • Between a food company and the public
   • Between the government and the public
   • Between employers and employees
   • In the home
   • Between staff and students at school/college
   • Between a doctor and patient.
5. Is there ever a danger of too much communication?

Chapter 2 Perception and Culture

Perception

Perception is the way we select, organise and interpret information about the world around us and that information comes to us through our five senses.

Fig. 2.1
'The wife and the mother-in-law'
by W.H. Hill

There are two points to be made here. First, perception starts with our five senses: sight, hearing, smell, touch and taste, and our senses are not always one hundred percent reliable. Railway tracks appear to get narrower as they get further away; a straight stick appears to bend in water; an ambulance siren changes tone as it moves past us. Second we all perceive things slightly differently from one another. Some people have better sight than others. A ferociously hot curry to one person may be mild to another. Deafening music to one person may be too quiet to another. This is called sensory variation.

Discussion

Our perception influences how we communicate and if we perceive things differently from others, we may run into communication problems. Discuss how you think this might occur.

Selection

We don't perceive everything that is going on around us, otherwise we would be bombarded by unnecessary information. So we only select what we need at a particular moment and the rest we filter out. Think of things you notice on the way to college. What do you perceive where you are sitting right now? Why do we select some things and fail to notice others?

Once we've perceived and selected something via our senses, we organise it to make sense of it, and we do this depending on our own background, experience, education and culture. Since we all have different experiences we won't always agree on what something *means*, and this can naturally lead to communication difficulties.

Discussion

It is possible to train the senses to become more effective. Visually impaired people may develop better hearing, smell and sense of touch than people who can see. Certain occupations need well-trained senses. Can you think of a few?

People Perception

The most important type of perception for a course in communication is people perception.

When we meet people initially, we perceive them based on their appearance and the role they are playing, and we match it to our own expectations and experience. We begin to weigh them up and make assumptions about them. We categorise them and put them in a box based on our perception. Categorising is a useful tool as it enables us to label things and make sense of the world. Unfortunately, people are far more complex than things and we cannot use such a simple system of classification for perceiving them. The worst kind of categorising is stereotyping.

Stereotyping

As a simple and convenient way of trying to understand the world, stereotyping can be useful. We stereotype objects, situations and people based on how we think they will live up to our expectations of them. Sometimes they are accurate and sometimes they aren't. Stereotypes are generalisations, sometimes based on facts that are generally true about a group. They can also be based upon assumptions instead of facts.

Prejudice

Prejudice is our attitude towards a group or individual without having adequate knowledge of either and stemming from a stereotype, preconceived opinion or inaccurate perception. However, as the old saying goes: we can't judge a book by its cover.

Perception and communication are very much intertwined. On the one hand, perception influences how we communicate, for example, if we perceive someone as being authoritative and we admire them we'll probably communicate with them in a respectful way. If we perceive someone as being stupid or worthless we will probably communicate with them less than respectfully! On the other hand, communication influences our perception of others. The way someone talks, their accent, their articulation, their pitch and tone of voice can often shape our opinion and our perception of them.

Discussion

Describe an occasion when your initial perceptions of someone were totally wrong.

Fig. 2.2

What are your first impressions of the people in the photographs in Figure 2.2? Explain why.

Culture

Culture is the set of beliefs, values, understandings, practises and ways of making sense of the world that are shared by a group of people. The culture in which we are brought up determines our thinking, our behaviour, our perceptions and how we communicate.

Discussion

What attributes do you think are a part of Irish culture? How many of them are stereotypes? What other Irish stereotypes are there? How do non-Irish members of the class group perceive Irish cultural values and norms?

Activity

Individually, write down three ways you think you fit into your cultural stereotype and three ways you think you don't. Discuss as a class group.

When we speak about Irish culture we often think of Celtic influences, because the Irish language is a Celtic language. However, Irish culture is a mixture of pre-Celtic, Celtic, Viking, Norman, English, Scottish and American cultural influences. Today, many people from all over Europe, Africa and Asia are coming to live in Ireland, adding to the already interesting mixture. Ireland is a multicultural society, and this cultural diversity is a source of richness for society.

In such a culturally diverse world, we come into contact with people with hugely different experiences and backgrounds from our own in terms of their ethnic group, religious beliefs, skin colour, sexual orientation, etc. To avoid misunderstandings we need to be aware of the differences in how they communicate.

Discussion

In what ways do people from different cultural backgrounds communicate differently?

How we communicate with each other defines the culture to which we belong and in turn, our culture determines how we communicate. The language and expressions we use every day reveal our cultural origins, for example, 'I'm after eating my tea,' is English but is a direct translation of an Irish idiom, and would not be found in other English speaking countries. This is sometimes called Hiberno-English.

Discussion

1. What other expressions and words are particular to Ireland? Would a visitor from another culture find it easy to understand these expressions even if she spoke English?
2. Proverbs, sayings and clichés illustrate how communication can define culture. Think of some Irish proverbs, sayings or clichés that underpin aspects of Irish culture. What do they say about the values and beliefs of Irish culture? For example, 'May you be in heaven half an hour before the devil knows you're dead,' shows the traditional Irish belief in heaven and the devil and perhaps the value of trickery. Non-Irish students in the class group could share their own proverbs.

Social Communities

A minority culture can also exist within a larger dominant culture. Such groups of people are called social communities. Social communities may be defined by countries of origin, for example, the Romanian community in Ireland, but also by their different ways of communicating and behaving. One of the most important types of social community to which everyone belongs is our gender.

Gender

The words gender and sex are often used interchangeably, but whereas sex relates to biological differences, gender refers to what society considers to be appropriate masculine and feminine behaviour at a given time. For example, in Irish society it is generally considered inappropriate for businessmen to wear skirts. In one hundred years' time it might become perfectly acceptable. Different cultures would have different norms regarding gender behaviour. However, it is possible for a woman to exhibit behaviour and communication traits traditionally considered to be masculine, even though she belongs to the female sex, and vice versa.

Discussion
In what ways do men and women communicate differently/similarly?

Socialisation

Socialisation is the process by which we learn to fit in to our society and culture and the rules and expectations that govern each of those. We learn through relationships and experience how to behave appropriately in a variety of situations and communication is a vital part of that process.

Studies have shown that in Western society boys and girls are socialised differently in the games they play. Girls tend to play games that involve cooperation and talk such as house and school. Boys usually are more competitive and action-orientated and play at war and team sports.

These rules of play often continue later in life and women tend to communicate more expressively, talk about feelings and relationships and tend to see talking as vital in making and sustaining relationships. Men are usually more competitive in their communication, focussed on tasks and activities, preferring to do things with their friends and partners.

It must be stressed that the following differences between feminine and masculine communication traits don't apply solely to women and men respectively. Most people would have a mixture from each list and this is perfectly normal and sometimes preferable. Some men might even display more feminine ways of communication than women and some women may communicate more masculine traits than men. It is important here not to fall into the trap of stereotyping. *Feminine communication* in general:

- Includes and shows interest in others
- Is co-operative
- Observes turn taking in speech
- Is responsive to what others say
- Uses talk expressively – talk deals with feelings, personal ideas, and problems, and is used to build relationships with others
- Seeks approval and wants to be liked by others
- Is better in private conversations and dialogue
- Asks questions to make connections, to lessen the potential for disagreement and to seek information that shows respect for another's knowledge.

Masculine communication in general
- Is self assertive and competitive
- Uses talk to establish identity, expertise, and knowledge, to prove oneself, to seek status and maintain independence
- Uses talk to gain and hold attention, to take the talk stage from others, interrupt and reroute topics to keep the focus on oneself and one's ideas
- Uses talk instrumentally – talk accomplishes something such as solving a problem, giving advice, or taking a stand on issues
- Involves stories and jokes in an attempt to be the funniest, cleverest etc.
- Is better in public situations and monologue
- Doesn't like to ask questions as it shows a lack of self-sufficiency and independence and a loss of face
- Asks questions as a way of arguing.

(Adapted from Julia Wood *Communication in Our Lives*, p. 91)

In positions of leadership, women tend to downplay their authority by seeking feedback, asking questions and expressing more doubt than men. They are unlikely to draw attention to their achievements or to their trappings of success as much as men. Compared to men, they will praise others more, apologise and accept blame more. As leaders, men generally downplay their faults and weaknesses, and see how another's position of power might affect their power.

Both feminine and masculine ways of communicating are equally valid, and neither is right or wrong. By being aware of these differences and by practising some of the styles of communication of the opposite gender many misunderstandings can be avoided.

Activity

Are the following typically masculine or feminine statements:
1. I'm sorry to hear about your illness. How are you feeling now?
2. So you lost your bet on the game. I won £70.
3. I'm going to apply for that managerial job. Do you think I have a chance?
4. Nice hat. Pity about the colour. Check mine out.

5. You've had your hair done. It's gorgeous!
6. I've been feeling very vulnerable lately.
7. I've always said that economic growth wouldn't last that long and I was right.
8. I like the shape of the windows, what do you think?
9. In my view, they're the best band around at the moment, no argument.
10. I'm sorry about the way I went on last night. I won't do it again.

Activity

In social and vocational situations observe a group of people having a conversation/discussion and note the gender differences in communication styles.

For Reflection

Observe yourself in social and vocational situations and how you interact with different groups of people. Do you exhibit predominantly masculine or feminine ways of communication?

We often experience pressure to conform to standards of masculinity and femininity, so that men are sometimes afraid of appearing effeminate and women of being 'butch'. However the most effective communicators are equally comfortable using both ways of communicating.

Other Social Communities

Discussion

1. What other social communities exist in Ireland? They might be based on religious beliefs, ethnic origins, sexual orientation, social class, age or disabilities. Identify two positive and two negative stereotypes you have for each of the social communities you thought of.
2. What do you understand by the following terms:
   (a) Sexism
   (b) Ageism
   (c) Homophobia
   (d) Discrimination

Fig 2.3

What is the purpose of the advertisement in Figure 2.3? Do you think it works? Why?

Handicapped is a term that was once used to describe disabled people. It is now considered offensive because it refers to begging: 'cap in hand', which is how many disabled people survived in former times.

Xenophobia (pronounced 'zen')

Xenophobia is the fear and dislike of strangers. In primitive times this was useful because it lessened the likelihood of being captured or killed by rival tribes.

Ethnocentrism

Ethnocentrism is the belief that our own culture or ethnic group is at the centre of the world, is normal or even superior and that others are strange or inferior.

Racism

Extreme ethnocentrism is sometimes called racism in which one group thinks it is so superior that it dominates, suppresses and even destroys other ethnic groups. The idea of race as something biological, genetic or physiological has no scientific foundation whatsoever even though the word has often been used to refer to groups of people based on their skin colour, religious beliefs or culture. Recent genetic studies have shown that it is possible for a white Irish person to be genetically closer to a black African than to another white Irish person.

Fig. 2.4 Chain racism.

Sectarianism

Sectarianism is prejudice against people who belong to a different sect, or religious denomination. In Ireland this has particular resonance, because intolerance has been displayed between some individuals belonging to the Roman Catholic Church and some from the Protestant Church for many years. To many observers, it is ironic because both belong to the same Christian religion.

Sectarianism occurs in many parts of the world where groups belonging to different religious beliefs live next to each other.

Discussion

Think of and discuss examples of communication or behaviour that you consider to be racist and that you consider to be sectarian.

We can reduce ethnocentrism, racism and sectarianism by understanding that cultures vary in their beliefs, values and behaviour, and no one culture is the normal or right one. For example, we might find it strange that Jewish people don't eat pork or that Hindus don't eat beef. But the French might find it odd that we don't eat horsemeat. Some people find it peculiar that vegetarians don't eat any meat at all.

Improving Intercultural Communication

Most of us spend most of the time with people from our own culture and social communities. We can communicate easily in these groups because we have shared understandings about appropriate language and behaviour. When we encounter people from other social and cultural groups we don't have the same guidelines. Researchers have come up with a process, which consists of five levels of response to cultural diversity. It can help develop an awareness of other cultures and minimise misunderstandings. It can take time to go from one stage to the next and some people will take to it more quickly and easily than others. Ultimately, it should reduce our ethnocentrism and improve our intercultural communication skills.

1. Resistance

This occurs when we attack other cultures' practices as being inferior to our own. Sometimes groups are forced to give up their own practices in order to assimilate into a dominant culture. Level one is recognising our own ethnocentrism. We might believe our culture is the best, but that is merely an opinion, not a fact.

2. Tolerance

This is when we accept and tolerate differences of other groups, even though we might not understand or approve of them. We may still assume our ways are the standard and that others are somehow inferior. Level two is avoiding criticism of other cultures.

3. Understanding

At this stage we attempt to understand the values and beliefs of other cultures because we realise that there are various reasons why some social communities have different practises from our own.

4. Respect

At this level we begin to see others for what they are and appreciate their differences. If we show respect for people from other cultures, they will do the same to us.

5. Participation

The final level in this process is when we actively participate in some activity of another culture. We become 'multilingual' in that we can communicate with a variety of social communities without losing our own identity. Many immigrants in Ireland are already bilingual in that they can speak their own language but in order to fit in to the dominant culture they have learnt English. At this stage we can focus on individual people not cultures. Each culture is made up of individuals who all think and behave differently from each other. They won't all conform to stereotypes!

For Reflection

Consider at which level you operate and try to progress to the next level.

By remaining stuck in our own culture's way of living we not only miss out on the richness of life but we also maintain a very narrow way of communicating. At some point we are going to meet people very different from ourselves and we need to be able to communicate with them comfortably and effectively.

Discussion

Have you ever experienced prejudice because of your particular culture or social community? Discuss your experience with the class group.

Due to the power that language can have, some say it can be misused to legitimise dominant cultures and to label other cultures as inferior. Political correctness refers to language and behaviour that avoids causing offence to social communities and disadvantaged people. Whereas many of these terms succeed and are appropriate, many are over the top and even bizarre. Many find 'male nurse' and 'lady doctor' offensive. In Ireland 'Travellers' has replaced 'Itinerants' and 'Tinkers'. Members of a group have a right to be called by a collective name with which they are comfortable.

Discussion

What groups do you think the following terms apply to:
• African American
• Visually impaired
• Follically challenged
• Socially misaligned
• Senior citizens
• Mentally challenged
• Native American
• Aesthetically challenged
• Flight attendants
• Vocally challenged
• Utensil sanitizer
• Non human companions
Can you explain the reason for the above words? Which do you find appropriate and which are over the top? What about the use of 'person' instead of 'man' as a suffix, e.g. chairperson, postperson, fireperson? Think of other examples and discuss whether you find them appropriate or not.

Chapter Review

1. Explain how misperception can lead to communication problems.
2. Explain the role of sensory variation in the process of perception.
3. What does selection mean?
4. What is the significance of stereotyping in relation to perception?
5. What is culture? How does it affect the way we perceive and communicate?
6. Explain the concept of socialisation.
7. What is a social community?
8. What are the main differences between the way men and women communicate?
9. Explain the following:
   • Cultural diversity
   • Xenophobia
   • Ethnocentrism
   • Racism.
10. Outline the five stages for reducing ethnocentrism and improving intercultural skills.

Part 2 The Written
Word

Chapter 3 Reading

 Purpose of Reading

Discussion

What do we read and why? Discuss the types of things you have read in the past twenty-four hours.

We read primarily for the following reasons:
1. Information
2. Entertainment/leisure
3. Personal contact
4. Education.

There is another very sound reason to read. It improves our command of the language we speak by increasing our vocabulary and this in turn helps improve our communication skills. Reading helps us to expand our range of words so that we can express ourselves more eloquently.

Our reading will improve by practice and our communication skills will improve by reading. Although it is tempting to take the easy way out and read what is unchallenging, we won't improve unless we read material that introduces us to new words and new ways of expression. Reading regularly and widely is the main thing. Don't always read the same type of material. If you've been used to magazines, try a newspaper. If you read novels, try a work of non-fiction. If non-fiction is your thing, try a comic for a change.

It is also useful to have a good dictionary at hand to look up new words.

HAGAR THE HORRIBLE

Fig. 3.1

Reading Self-check

How well do you read? We all read at varying speeds and levels of concentration and efficiency. Here are some of the most common problems that people have with reading:

1. Reading all kinds of text at the same speed.

2. Slow reading.

3. Re-reading words or passages.

4. Inability to find the main idea in a passage.

5. Losing concentration while reading.

6. Pronouncing or mouthing words while reading them.

7. Study-reading intensely for a long period of time without taking a break.

If you do any or all of the above you have developed some bad habits over the years, but by and large they are problems that can be overcome with a little effort. In the following few pages we will look at some of the ways in which our reading can be improved.

Different Texts Different Speeds

If you think about what you've read in the past twenty-four hours you will notice the sheer variety of texts. We don't use the same method of reading for all of them. For example, when looking at a bus timetable we don't read every single word on the page. We scan it for the particular item relevant to us. We would use a different method for reading a novel. With a novel we would read every word but not as intensely as if we were studying a book for an exam.

Types of Reading

There are four types of reading:

1. Scanning

2. Skimming

3. Normal reading

4. Close reading

Scanning

This is very fast reading to find specific information that is only relevant to our needs. We scan timetables, dictionaries, small ads, notice boards and telephone directories for specific words or names. We scan newspapers for articles that interest us and web pages on the Internet for relevant pieces of information or for links to other pages. Scanning is useful for finding information as part of a research project.

Activity

You've decided you want to learn how to swim so you get a brochure from the local pool. Scan the timetable of the various sessions to find a suitable time for a lesson. Your working hours are 9.00 am till 5.00 pm. Monday till Saturday with Wednesdays free, and you work till 8.30 pm on Tuesdays.

	Monday	Tuesday	Wednesday	Thursday	Friday	Saturday	Sunday
7.30	Early Swim	Early Swim	Early Swim	Early Swim	Early Swim	Closed	Closed
9.00	Open Swim	Open Swim	Adults	Open Swim	Adults	Closed	Closed
10.00			AdultLesson	ChildLesson	ChildLesson	Family	Closed
11.00	Open Swim	Club	Club	Open Swim	Club	ChildLesson	Family
12.00						ChildLesson	Family
13.00	Lunch Swim	Lunch Swim	Lunch Swim	Lunch Swim	Lunch Swim	Adults	Family
14.00						Open Swim	Open Swim
15.00	ChildLesson					Open Swim	Open Swim
16.00	Open Swim	Family	ChildLesson	ChildLesson		Open Swim	Open Swim
17.00	Open Swim	Lane Swim	Open Swim	Lane Swim	Open Swim	Open Swim	Open Swim
18.00	Family	Open Swim	Family	Open Swim	Family	Closed	Closed
19.00	Club	Club	ChildLesson	Club	Club		
20.00	AdultLesson	AdultLesson	Club	Open Swim	Open Swim		
21.00	Adults	Adults	Club	Adults	Adults		

How did you scan the timetable? Did you do it methodically starting from Monday at 7.30 am and carefully work your way down each day? Or did you scan it haphazardly looking all over the place with no apparent system? Having a methodical system can sometimes help us find information more quickly.

Skimming

When we skim read a passage we swiftly glance across the surface to get an overview of what it is about. Passages may be skipped because they are irrelevant. We skim advertisements, newspaper articles and brochures. For study or research purposes a skim read lets us know if the material is relevant to our needs, and if it is, we can then go back and read it in detail. Topic sentences are often placed either at the beginning or at the end of paragraphs. When skimming we can focus on these to get the gist of the text. It is good to skim read any piece of writing before reading it fully. Then when we go to read it at a normal pace we will absorb the information more easily.

Signposts

In most textbooks and some news articles, headings, subheadings and headlines indicate what is to follow in the main body of the text, acting as signposts. Words and phrases that are underlined, in **bold**, in *italics*, numbered, lettered or in bullet points are often signposts and are easily skim read.

Normal Reading

This is reading at moderate speed, for example: novels, letters, newspaper articles and magazines. A lack of speed is considered to be a major reading problem. It is often found that with increased speed comes better understanding. The average person reads at about 240 words per minute with a comprehension rate of about 60%. This means that most of us do not remember 40% of what we read. If we assume that we are average readers and we practise reading everyday, we are still well behind the most efficient readers, who can read around 1000 words per minute with an 85% comprehension rate. Most of us could do with improvement in both our speed and comprehension. If you are curious about your reading speed, there is a free test at either of the following websites:

☀ http://www.readingsoft.com/ or

☀ http://www.speedreading2000.com/readtest.htm.

When we read, our eyes do not move smoothly across the page from left to right, because every now and then they stop very briefly to take in a word or a phrase. These stops are called *fixations* and normally last between one quarter to one and a half seconds. The number of words we focus on during each fixation is referred to as the *recognition span*. Fast readers can read vertically down a page, fixating on each line just once and taking in its whole meaning. These people have a large recognition span. So, obviously the greater the recognition span, the fewer fixations we need and the faster we will read. Slower readers make more fixations because they have a smaller recognition span. Unfortunately, meaning in sentences does not come in single words but in chunks of words, phrases and sentences. When we try to take in meaning, one word at a time, by the time we reach the end of a sentence we have forgotten what was at the beginning. Because the human brain can function much faster than this, we are leaving time for our mind to drift off and think about something else. So, we lose concentration and start to daydream.

Activity

Read the following passage slowly, one word at a time, covering up each word in front of the one you are reading:

In...spite...of...what...you...might...think...reading...can...be...improved ...by...fixating...on...groups...of...words...rather...than...on...single...wo rds...because...single...words...don't...mean...much...on...their...own.

As you will have noticed, this very slow way of reading makes it more difficult to understand the sentence quickly. We don't find any meaning at all in the first few words and things only start to make sense once we reach the word 'improved'. A more efficient reader will read the sentence in clusters of meaning like this:

In spite of what you might think...reading can be improved...by fixating on groups of words...rather than on single words...because single words don't mean much on their own.

We need to push ourselves to practise reducing our fixation time, and at the same time try to expand our recognition span. This should increase our speed, our comprehension and also help reduce concentration loss.

Re-reading

Re-reading words or phrases in a passage naturally decreases our reading efficiency. To reduce this habit we can use a pointer when reading. This might seem a little childish, but it helps our eyes move more smoothly across the page. Alternately, we can cover up the lines already read with a sheet of paper, card or another book, and even push it down a little faster than we think we can go. This means we will concentrate better on what we are reading the first time and it helps us break the habit.

These techniques should be practised regularly for our reading efficiency to improve.

Close Reading

This is reading which is slow and intensive because the text is demanding and needs to be properly understood. We might close read poetry, class notes, textbooks, instructions for operating equipment or for examinations, leases, contracts and other detailed documents so that we understand them fully.

It is not a good idea to read long difficult passages for more than about forty minutes at a time. After this time we tend to lose our ability to concentrate, and a short break of five to ten minutes is usually sufficient to refresh ourselves.

Tips for Close Reading

1. Have a pen, paper and dictionary handy.
2. Start with a skim read of the entire passage. If it's a book, look at the title, contents, introduction, conclusion, heading and subheadings. Scan the index for specific subjects.
3. Read the passage *actively*. This means asking yourself questions such as:
    (a) 'Why is it written this way?'
    (b) 'What does the writer mean by this?'
    (c) 'Do I agree with this?'
    (d) 'Do I find this information new, interesting, boring?'
    (e) 'What are the main points?'
4. Note information that you already know.
5. Note information that you find particularly interesting, relevant, irrelevant, or even ridiculous.

6. Write down, highlight or underline difficult words or passages.
7. Look up any unfamiliar words.
8. When you've read the passage, try to recall it in your mind. What are the main points of the passage? Write down what you can remember in your own words.
9. Finally go over the passage again in case you've missed any important points.

Activity

Read the following article, using all four methods of reading. Scan it first for words you don't understand and underline them. Look them up in a dictionary or consult your tutor. Skim the article to get the gist of what it's about. Read it normally to get the details and finally close read it to see if you can work out any further meanings, and to examine its style. What do you think of the ideas in the piece? Is it well written? Can you comment on the writer's style? Finally, write a summary paragraph including its main points.

More to Male Bonding than Beer and Football

From a woman's point of view, friendship keeps you emotionally healthy. And that's not a subjective opinion. Scientific studies have proven friendship can protect against psychological problems. But friendship can be a problem for men. Many men are so reliant on the women in their lives to provide a social environment for them that they have no other resources on which to fall back if the relationship fails. 'If you're in a relationship, your friends are your partner's friends too. When the relationship breaks up, men seem to lose all their friends,' says Conor, a separated man in his 30s.

Billy (50), a rigger in RTÉ, comments: 'When you marry, all your old friends are left behind and you go into your wife's circle of friends. Men are also very competitive, so that they are always looking at each other to see who is earning the most and who has the best car so it is impossible to get past that.

'I have male acquaintances that I drink with, sail with and go to matches with, but they are not friends. I have met my brothers for a pint, but that connection has fallen off and there is a distance there. Am I lonely? You could call it that. A real deep-down friendship is hard to find,' he says.

What is it about men and friendship? Michael Hardiman, psychologist and author, says: 'A lot of men find it difficult to experience the benefits of deep friendship. They may feel great affection and loyalty, but tend not to express it. Men have permission to express their feelings for one another only in situations of great adversity and danger, such as war. All the research into heroism shows that men are protecting each other, rather than fighting for a cause. 'When men are allowed to show fear and vulnerability, then the deepest connections can be expressed. Otherwise, men find it difficult to express friendship directly. Men can build extraordinarily deep bonds, but they don't name them. It's taboo to name your feelings.'

But men are changing. Fifteen years ago, TV footage of football matches would show men shaking hands, at most, in the moment of victory. Today men dance around, hug one another and even plant kisses on each other's lips. But such affection is permissible only on the sports field; it still doesn't mean that men are sharing their souls with each other. 'In Western culture, physical affection between men is taboo except in extraordinary situations,' says Hardiman.

For a woman to spend an evening as men do, in the company of friends gossiping about sports, business, cars and who is earning what, without any reference to their interior lives, would be regarded as rather cold. However, Rob Weatherill, psychologist and author, thinks that women are judging male friendship according to female standards. He doesn't see why men should have to disclose their souls the way women do if that doesn't feel right for them. 'Men have their own ways of being intimate with one another and they shouldn't be judged according to women's perceptions,' he argues.

Many men get around the male-to-male barrier by having their deepest friendships with women. 'Some of my friends would be female and I learn considerably more from them than I do from my male friends,' says John, a single man in his 20s. So is the psychological safety valve for men friendship with women? Maybe that's unfair, as illustrated by the following anecdote. Two men, both in their 40s, had experienced similar life threatening illnesses but had not discussed their experiences, as women would, with friends. Their wives arranged for them to meet and talk. The men talked about football, music, their college days and property prices, but not a mention was made of their shared crises. The wives thought the conversation had been a loss, but a few days later, both men confided that the conversation had made them feel much better. Perhaps there is an elegant, dignified mystery of male intimacy which women cannot judge by their own standards, in which the most important, intimate exchanges are contained in what is left unsaid.

Kathryn Holmquist,
The Irish Times, 12 September 2000.

Activities

1. Select a newspaper article and close read it using the guidelines above. When you've finished, recall the main points to the class group.
2. Reading for leisure can be one of the most satisfying of pastimes. Find out from your class what books people are reading or have recently read and make a list of them. Get each to give a brief review or recommendation of one book. Select from the recommendations three books that you will read during the next year. Use this as a way of starting a book club in your class/college. Avoid books that you studied in secondary school.

Chapter Review

1. Give four good reasons for reading.
2. List five bad reading habits.
3. Explain the four types of reading.
4. What does active reading mean?
5. Give a brief explanation of:
   (a) Signposts
   (b) Fixation
   (c) Recognition span

Chapter 4 Personal Writing

 Writing as a Response

Writing is often done in response to something. Personal writing can be a response to something we've experienced or felt. We might be responding to our own emotions, thoughts or experiences and we express them in poetry, a story, diary etc. Or we could be responding to events in society that prompt us to write a letter to a newspaper. A letter of thanks is a response to a favour done or gift received; a review is our response to a film, book, play etc. Functional writing could be in response to a brief we might have been given by an employer or a college tutor.

Personal Writing

Personal writing is about expressing our own personal experiences, thoughts and feelings. In effect we are communicating our personalities, which should come across in a piece of writing whether it be a letter, poem, story, review etc. It may also stem from simply reflecting on our lives, the lives of others or the world at large and expressing these reflections in writing.

Some people keep journals or diaries in which they regularly express their innermost thoughts and desires. This type of writing can be therapeutic and liberating, helping to unload psychological burdens that we may be carrying. Since we are doing it purely for ourselves it doesn't matter if its grammar or punctuation is weak.

Preparation

No matter what type of personal writing we are faced with, we all begin with the dreaded blank page and a head bereft of fresh ideas. How do we start? First of all we need to be clear *what* we are writing:

1. *Purpose/intention:* What do we want to achieve; what effect do we want to have on the reader?
2. *Topic:* What is it going to be about?
3. *Form:* What way is it going to be written - a poem, prose, story or dialogue? This will be strongly influenced by our purpose.
4. *Language:* The kinds of words we use will create the style, e.g. language using imagery and metaphor suits poetry but not a letter of application.
5. *Personal style:* Certain words or expressions that we commonly use and even the kind of sentence structure we usually employ (long/short etc.) denote our own particular style.
6. *Punctuation and grammar:* Obviously these need to be correct. (See Chapter 9.)

There are several stages we need to go through to put together a piece of writing:

Plan/Rough Notes

We cannot hope to write a piece from scratch and submit it as it is. There will always be mistakes and room for improvement. A brainstorming session to get all our ideas on the topic down onto a page is useful. We can then link them together by sub-topic (see page 183).

Draft

We then try to organise these notes to give them some kind of shape. We work out how to order each idea, how to begin and end the written piece and how we structure the main points in between.

Redraft/Edit

We might find some words we don't like. We might change them, make additions, omissions, polish, refine etc.

Proofread

It is wise to get someone else to proofread our work, as he will see the mistakes that we don't notice.

Where Do We Get Our Ideas?

Memory is one source of ideas. Experts often say, 'Write what you know.' If we can tap into our memory for experiences, events etc. we will be truly communicating our own personality.

Imagination – we can imagine scenarios, characters, situations and build a story around them.

Observation – look around you and write about what you see: people, nature, objects, events etc.

Some people are naturally more imaginative than others and have no problem finding inspiration to write. If we feel we aren't that imaginative or creative, writing a review in response to a film or book, or a letter in response to an event might be an easier option for a personal writing assignment. Remember that a tutor will have to read any number of pieces of personal writing so you should strive for some originality.

 # Short Story

Telling a story is not as easy as it might at first seem. A good story needs to hold the reader's attention and make her want to read on to find out what happens at the end. Sometimes the best stories are the ones we have experienced ourselves. We can always adapt them to make them more exciting and dramatic.

Techniques for Effective Narration

1. *Create a setting,* i.e. a time and a place. This can help with the mood, e.g. 'A dark stormy night in the woods,' evokes a very different mood from 'A sunny afternoon by the sea.'
2. *Create believable characters*, ideally based on real people that you know or have observed. Basing characters on real ones can be easier and sometimes the results are more realistic. The better the characters the more the reader will care about what happens to them. If the reader has no concern with them she might not want to finish the story. Characters are drawn by how they appear physically, what they do, what they say and how they say it. They might have little quirks that make them stand out from other characters and make them unique. The main character(s) should go through some kind of change, be it physical, emotional, spiritual or psychological, and emerge different at the end.
3. *Give the story a structure* that contains a sequence of events. The traditional beginning, middle and end need not come in that particular order.
4. *Give it a plot* that holds the reader's attention. Suspense, drama and conflict all hold the reader's attention. Get the characters to do things. Make things happen to them. A standard plot is: a situation causes an action, which meets complications, reaches a climax and is worked out at a resolution/closure. The simpler the plot, the better. Remember it is a *short* story.
5. Use a *variety of writing forms*, e.g. dialogue to make the characters come alive, description to give it detail and action to create suspense, drama, conflict etc.
6. Decide on the *type of narration* you will use. A first person narrator, in which the narrator is part of the story, can make it sound more personal and believable as the story sounds like it is

coming from someone who experienced the events first hand. Third person narration gives it a more objective, detached feel.

Activity

Read this short story and discuss the setting, characters, structure, plot, narration, language etc. It illustrates how short and simple an effective story can be. What is your opinion of it?

Angel

Sitting on the drippy, cold steps of Penn Station, sharing a smoke with a boyfriend. This Saturday night is scattered with drunks, and for once, we are not the drunkest; we do not smell the worst. Late-night, paranoid tourists don't even stare---a few ask for directions. We are spreading our wet, waiting bodies all over that stone, watching stumbling silhouettes wrestle with the escalator. She shuffles up the steps with the last of her strength. Her pink sweatpants are tinged with brown, and her feet are buried in city-stained bunny slippers. Her eyes look like they've seen so much sadness they're forever doomed to apathy. They are eyes dazed with the work it takes to stay warm, and weary of the excess of privileged people. I'm looking at those glass eyes and thinking that she reeks of survival; that I'm too cold to move, and all I'm doing is waiting for the first train home. Out comes her wrinkled, begging hand. We turn out our pockets and find nothing. The mouth of the station swallows her descending, dejected frame. Light another smoke. We are pushing reluctant time forward as it digs its heels in at the dusty smells and sounds of old stories, at the sucking of smoke, at our involuntary shivers. She's back again. The wrinkled hand, heavy with pleading, is now answering. She drops four warm quarters into my palm and says, "Get yourselves a cup of coffee. Merry Christmas." The station gulps her up again before we can say thank you.

Maria Raha
1999 from *www.storybytes.com*

✎ Poetry

We often think of poems being about miserable, lonely, heartbroken existences, but in fact poetry can be about anything and can be written in a variety of styles including dialogue and free verse (no formal structure).

If you haven't written poetry before, it's probably not a good idea to submit your first one for a communications assignment. A poem should have something special that will inspire the reader. This could include any or all of the following:

1. Language that is clever, beautiful, rhythmic, humorous or that uses sounds to good effect. Typical conventions are: assonance, alliteration, onomatopoeia and rhyme.

2. Imagery that the reader can 'see'. Metaphors and similes are useful for creating effective imagery.
3. Emotions that will inspire, move or entertain the reader.
4. Ideas that will provoke thought.

As with all personal writing, you should tap into your own memories and experiences for subject matter.

Activity

Read this poem by Seamus Heaney and consider the use of memory, observation and the senses as writing aids. Look also at his use of imagery, sounds and language. What does the poet say about poetry?

Digging

Between my finger and my thumb
The squat pen rests: snug as a gun.
Under my window, a clean rasping sound
When the spade sinks into gravelly ground:
My father, digging. I look down
Till his straining rump among the flowerbeds
Bends low, comes up twenty years away
Stooping in rhythm through potato drills
Where he was digging.
The coarse boot nestled on the lug, the shaft against the inside knee was
    levered firmly.
He rooted out tall tops, buried the bright edge deep
To scatter new potatoes that we picked
Loving their cool hardness in our hands.
By God, the old man could handle a spade.
Just like his old man.

The cold smell of potato mould, the squelch and slap
Of soggy peat, the curt cuts of an edge
Through living roots awaken in my head.
But I've no spade to follow men like them.
Between my finger and my thumb
The squat pen rests.
I'll dig with it.

Seamus Heaney
1966 from Death of a Naturalist.

Review

The purpose of a review is to give an *informed* opinion and criticism of a book, play, film, CD or concert. There should be sufficient detail to let the reader decide whether or not he wants to go and see/buy it. A film review, for example, should contain information about the following:

- *Director* – has he created a good film? How?
- *Actors* – have they played their parts well?
- *Characters* – are they believable, heroic, evil, etc.?
- *Plot* – is it exciting, suspenseful, realistic? The ending should not be revealed.
- *Setting* – where and when does it take place?
- *Genre* – what type of film is it: comedy, drama, science fiction, thriller etc. Is it a successful example of its genre?

Sometimes a film review might have further information about the budget, soundtrack, lighting, cinematography, special effects etc.

Activity

Read the following review of *The Dish* and discuss the various aspects of the film that are mentioned. Find examples of the writer's informed opinion. What evidence is there that the writer is an experienced reviewer?

The Dish

Director: Rob Sitch
Starring: Sam Neill, Patrick Warbuton, Kevin Harrington, Tom Long, Taylor Kane, Eliza Szonert
Details: Aus/104 mins/12s

July 1969. As the world prepares for the momentous event of the first men on the moon, the lives of the inhabitants of Parkes, an outback Australian town, are thrown into chaos. NASA has decided that their remote town is located in the optimum spot for beaming live pictures of the moonwalk around the globe. In the lead up to the massive event, the focus of the world is split between the men in space and the townsfolk responsible for ensuring that everyone can see pictures of them. Marshalling the town's efforts is the recently widowed Cliff Buxton (Sam Neill) but can he contend with the interfering busy bodies from the space agency, determined to run the show and claim all of the glory from the town's efforts?

Based on a true story, *The Dish* is a lightweight, though extremely enjoyable comedy on what happens to normal people in extraordinary situations. Like director Sitch's most recent effort *The Castle* (1997), plot matters and characters' development are sacrificed in favour of laughs. The characters are all painted with broad brush strokes but the material is as feel good as is humanly possibly. In lesser hands, it could have

Confusing Words

In each of the following sentences, select the correct word, decide what the other word means and put it into another sentence (it may have more than one meaning):

1. There is ample/amble opportunity to get to know each other.
2. Tourists can wonder/wander through the beautiful gardens at leisure.
3. She didn't except/accept my apology.
4. The film had a powerful effect/affect on me.
5. There was a full compliment/complement of members at the meeting.
6. He was completely disinterested/uninterested in the game.
7. There was a continuous/continual flow of water from the tap.
8. Don't loose/lose your keys.

Chapter 5 Letters

Personal Letters

With the arrival of new technologies, letter writing would appear to be a dying art. Today it seems much more efficient to send an email, text message or to telephone. Yet there is something special about receiving a personal letter from someone. A personal letter, be it a letter of thanks, condolence or congratulations, should be handwritten. Its purpose is to express personal thoughts, and if it is typed it becomes less personal, and the less personal, the less its effect. The receiver of a handwritten letter will note and appreciate personal touches.

Due to the nature of personal letters, their informality means that the rules are not as strict as for formal letters. Nevertheless a basic layout is required.

Layout of a Personal Letter

49 Bridge Street
Bray
Co. Wicklow

23 March 2002

Dear Philip

It's good to hear you've got yourself a new place to live. Your friend must have been getting sick of you living on her couch for the last three months.

I went to see Giant Sand last week with Hugh and they were absolutely brilliant. Shona got us free tickets and afterwards we went back to Sam and Eileen's for a poker session. You should have been there. Donal lost €20.

If I get a chance I'll come over and visit you in the summer. But you know how it is these days; helping Jake and Dorothy with the festival and all the animals. I'll let you know.

Hope you're keeping well.

All the best

Martin

The sender's address should go at the top right-hand side of the page. The date goes below this. The salutation begins below the date but on the left-hand side. Indent the first and all subsequent paragraphs. There are a variety of ways to close a personal letter depending on how well we know the recipient. 'Yours sincerely' may be too formal for some people. 'Yours affectionately' for close relations or friends, or simply 'Yours' for a close friend. For people we know well, familiar endings such as 'Love', 'All the best' or 'Best Wishes' are also typical.

Thanks

A letter of thanks is not only showing appreciation for a favour or a gift, but also acts as acknowledgment of receipt. It does not have to be very long, but should be sincere and contain a personal touch. It may be used as a reply to invitations, on receipt of gifts/presents, after weddings, parties and visits or in response to help given or acknowledgment of expressions of condolences. Two short paragraphs are sufficient.

Paragraph 1

Suggestions:

- 'Many thanks for the book you sent me. It was very kind of you. I haven't been able to put it down since...'
- 'Thank you very much for the wedding present you gave us. It is proving to be very useful.'

Paragraph 2

Could contain some simple news about yourself or about the receiver:

- 'It was good to see you...'
- 'I have been really busy lately, studying hard at college...'

Condolences

A letter of condolence can be a difficult and sensitive piece of writing. It is important to find the right amount of sincerity, without going over the top and sounding false. It should contain words of sympathy:

- 'I was sorry to hear about the death of...'
- 'We were so shocked to hear the sad news about...'

Words of Comfort

- 'She was a wonderful person, kind and generous...'
- 'We are thinking of you at this sad and difficult time'
- 'He was a great friend and will be greatly missed'

If practical, some offer of assistance:

- 'If there is anything I can do...'

To personalise a letter of condolence, we can include a personal memory we ourselves had of the deceased or an anecdote about a time spent in his company: 'I remember the time when...'

Congratulations

Offering congratulations is a simple matter and may be used for the following occasions: passing exams, engagement, wedding, promotion, birth of a child, a new home.

Some useful phrases:

- 'We wish you every success in your new position'
- 'I am delighted to hear the good news'
- 'We were overjoyed to hear the news about the birth of your son'
- 'You should be proud of such a fine achievement'
- 'Well done'
- 'Congratulations'

There is even scope here for humour such as:

'I never thought you had it in you' (not for the birth of a child!)

Formal/Business Letters

All formal and business letters should be typed/word-processed except for a job application letter. When typing a letter it is practical to use the fully blocked style. This is means everything, address, date, salutation etc. starts from the left-hand margin and is frequently used with open punctuation, in other words, only the body of the letter contains commas, full-stops etc. The style for business letters today is short and to the point.

Sample Business Letter

E–Zee
Internet Services and Web Design
31 Main Street
Kilkenny
Co. Kilkenny   1

056 2144781

Ref BO/RD   2

13 March 2002   3

Ms Tanya Fitzpatrick
Principal
Drumlinn College of Further Education   4
Drumlinn
Co. Monaghan

Re: Quotation for design of website   5

Dear Ms Fitzpatrick   6
Thank you for your enquiry of 4 March concerning our web design services which were   7
recently advertised in *The Irish Times*.

Although we are a relatively new company, we already have a reputation for a fast, efficient   7
service, state of the art technology and a design team, which has many years' experience.

I have consulted with my chief designer and am pleased to submit a quotation for the   7
requirements you outlined in your letter. I hope this meets with your approval.

Please do not hesitate to contact me if you require any further information.   7

Yours sincerely   8

Brian O'Neill   9

Brian O'Neill   10
Manager
Enc   11

Layout

The layout of a business letter is as follows:

1. The sender's address unless the paper has a company letterhead, which will include the address, phone number, fax and email address.
2. A reference which is used for filing purposes and is usually the sender's and typist's initials (optional).
3. The date like this: 9 March 2002. The 'th' after numbers is usually omitted these days and avoid abbreviations such as: 9/3/02.
4. The recipient's or inside name, title and address.
5. The heading if required: 'Re: Quotation for design of website'.
6. The salutation:
   - 'Dear Sir/Madam' (if the recipient is unknown)
   - 'Dear Sir' (if recipient is known to be male)
   - 'Dear Madam' (if recipient is known to be female)
   - 'Dear Mr/Mrs/Ms/Miss Fitzpatrick'
   - 'A Chara'.
7. The body of the letter. A simple rule is: keep it clear, concise and courteous. If it can be written in three paragraphs, that is enough, with one main idea per paragraph.

   The breakdown of the body of the letter should be as follows:
   - Paragraph 1: State the background or context of the letter, e.g.
     - 'Thank you for your letter of 13 July last in which you stated...'
     - 'I would like to apply for the post of…'
     - 'I would like an estimate for…'
   - Paragraph 2: The reason for writing, the 'main thrust' of the message.
   - Paragraph 3: Round off with an indication of an expected outcome, or further communication.
     - 'I look forward to hearing from you at your earliest convenience'
     - 'Please do not hesitate to contact me, should you require any additional information'.
8. Complimentary closure:
   - 'Yours faithfully' if begun with 'Dear Sir'/'Dear Madam'
   - 'Yours sincerely' if begun with 'Dear Mr'/'Ms' etc.
9. Signature (handwritten).
10. Name and title of signatory (typed/word-processed).
11. Enc for an enclosed document or Encs for more than one.
12. Cc if copies are being sent to other parties.

General Guidelines

1. Always make notes or do at least one rough draft before you start to write your letter.
2. Proofread.
3. Use an appropriate tone.

4. Spelling, grammar and punctuation should be accurate.
5. Use good quality paper and matching envelopes if possible.
6. Write on one side of the page only.
7. Keep copies of all letters you send.

 # Letter of Application

Despite the increase in email applications for jobs, many employers today still require a handwritten letter, where there is no formal application form. Handwriting may be the first obstacle to many of us when faced with this task. If our handwriting is weak, untidy or just illegible we need to improve it. The prospective employer, who must decide between two applicants of equal qualifications and skills, may well select the applicant who has sent a neat, well laid out letter. This may demonstrate that the applicant is more conscientious. A sloppily written letter often gives the impression that the writer is slapdash in his attitude, not something that employers are looking for. A letter of application is the first impression someone will get of us, so if it is well written and presented, it can be good for our reputation.

Breakdown of a Letter of Application

Paragraph 1
Be precise about the position for which you are applying and include where you read/heard about it.

Paragraph 2
Refer to your CV and add anything of particular relevance to the position for which you are applying.

Paragraph 3
Round off with a statement of expected outcome.

General Guidelines

1. Keep copies of all letters you send.
2. Before writing, find out details of the position for which you are applying.
3. If possible, find out the name of the person to whom you should apply and address the letter to that person.
4. Find out what they are looking for and sell yourself accordingly.
5. Be sincere, truthful and quietly confident.
6. Never send originals of references or certificates, always copies.

Sample Letter of Application

Riverside House
Bridge Street
Bandon
Co. Cork

(023) 496803
086 7724391

20 May 2002

Gerard Dalton
Manager
E-Zee
Internet Services and Web Design
22 Main Street
Cork
Co. Cork

Dear Mr Dalton

I would like to apply for the position of web designer, as advertised in The Irish Times on Friday 14th April.

I enclose a copy of my Curriculum Vitae, with the names of two referees.

I would like to draw your attention specifically to the work experience I did at Phantom Internet Services, as part of my course at Drumlinn College of Further Education last March.

I look forward to hearing from you, should you consider me suitable for interview.

Yours sincerely

Stephen Loughran

Enc

Other Formal Letters

Letter of Enquiry

1. Make sure you give complete and precise details about the information you require.
2. Ask someone to proofread your letter as if he is the recipient.

Reply to an Enquiry

1. Begin with a reference to the enquiry.
2. Information can be presented clearly by using numbered or bulleted headings.
3. As above, ask someone to proofread.

Letter of Complaint

1. Reasons for sending:
   - On receipt of shoddy goods
   - On receipt of poor service
   - Environmental nuisance/disturbance
   - To record your annoyance
   - To seek an end to a situation
   - To seek redress for damage/inconvenience caused
2. Always write a letter of complaint as soon as possible after the situation or event.
3. Start with statement of regret.
4. When complaining use a tone that is polite but firm.
5. Explain the inconvenience caused to you and the dissatisfaction you felt, using I-statements, not you-statements, e.g. 'I was very distressed...'
6. Avoid being offensive, rude or overly dramatic.
7. Supply details to support complaint – dates, times, numbers, documents etc.
8. Offer a suggestion of how the matter might be rectified either by compensation, replacement etc.

Letter of Adjustment (Reply to a complaint)

1. Whether a complaint is justified or not, be tactful.
2. If it is justified accept responsibility, offer an expression of regret, an explanation, an apology and an intention to rectify the matter by compensation etc.
3. If it is not justified (and be quite certain that it isn't), politely make this clear.
4. If a complaint is mishandled, it could result in loss of business, goodwill or adverse publicity.

Assessment Activities

1. Write a letter of thanks to your work experience employer.
2. Write a letter to a friend/relative offering condolences on the death of a close relative.
3. Write a letter of congratulations to a friend who has just got married/engaged/promoted/become a parent/passed an exam.

Confusing Words

In each of the following sentences, select the correct word, decide what the other word means
and put it into another sentence (it may have more than one meaning):

1. Write to the personal/personnel manager.
2. Who is the principle/principal of this college?
3. The forest was very quiet/quite at night-time.
4. No dogs are aloud/allowed.
5. The award ceremony will precede/proceed the speeches.
6. You can hire/higher a car at the airport.
7. It looked like a scene/seen out of a disaster movie.
8. The couple decided to steel/steal away in the dead of night.

Chapter 6 Functional Writing

FETAC Assessment Requirement
Business Documentation—memorandum

Topics Covered

Application Form

Curriculum Vitae

Memorandum

Functional writing requires a more formal approach with less room for self-expression or creativity than personal writing. Whereas personal writing gives us the opportunity to express our individual personalities, functional and vocational writing requires that we stick to specific standards, formats, layouts and use language that is impersonal, plain and direct.

Application Form

Filling in a job application form sounds simple enough but many opportunities are lost due to carelessness. Here are a few tips:

1. Make a photocopy of the original and fill it in first. If you make mistakes you can do it again.
2. Skim read the whole form before completing it.
3. Keep handwriting as neat and clear as possible.
4. Check all instructions, e.g. using block capitals, ink colour etc.
5. Don't rush it.
6. Double check all information you give for accuracy.
7. Include information that is accurate – you might have to explain it in an interview.
8. Get permission from referees before you use their names.
9. Get someone to proofread it when finished.
10. Make a photocopy of the completed form for your own use, e.g. to prepare for the interview.
11. Take the same care to address the envelope.

Sample Job Application Form

Surname: _____

First Name(s): _____

Sex: _____

Address: _____

_____

_____

Telephone Number: _____

Home address: _____

_____

_____

Telephone Number: _____

Mobile: _____

Email: _____

Date of Birth: _____

Nationality: _____

Do you have any physical disabilities? _____

If so, give details: _____

_____

_____

Have you ever suffered from any serious illnesses? _____

If so, give details: _____

_____

_____

Do you have a full current driving licence? _____

Have you ever been charged for a driving offence or been involved in a serious

   accident? _____

If so, give details: _____

_____

Have you ever been convicted for a criminal offence?_____

If so, give details: _____

_____

_____

Language proficiency: _____

Computer proficiency: _____

How did you learn about this vacancy? _____

Have you worked for this company before? _____

If so, when?_____

_____

_____

EDUCATION

List in chronological order.

Schools	Dates	Subjects	Results
_____	_____	_____	_____
_____	_____	_____	_____
_____	_____	_____	_____
_____	_____	_____	_____
_____	_____	_____	_____
_____	_____	_____	_____
_____	_____	_____	_____

College(s)	Dates	Course(s)	Results
_____	_____	_____	_____
_____	_____	_____	_____
_____	_____	_____	_____
_____	_____	_____	_____
_____	_____	_____	_____
_____	_____	_____	_____

EMPLOYMENT

Name and address of previous employer(s)	Dates	Position held	Reason for leaving
_____	_____	_____	_____
_____	_____	_____	_____
_____	_____	_____	_____
_____	_____	_____	_____
_____	_____	_____	_____
_____	_____	_____	_____
_____	_____	_____	_____

INTERESTS

Give details of any interests, pastimes and achievements:

_____

_____

_____

_____

Outline your reasons for wanting this position:

_____

_____

_____

_____

Additional information that you think might be relevant:

_____

_____

_____

_____

Please give names and addresses of two referees:

Name: _____

Address: _____

_____

_____

Telephone Number:_____

Name: _____

Address: _____

_____

_____

Telephone Number:_____

Signature: _____

Date:_____

Curriculum Vitae

Latin for 'Course of Life' a CV should be neatly presented and well laid out. There are various ways of presenting a CV, but if possible keep it to one page in length. It generally contains the following information:

• Personal Details
• Education
• Work Experience
• Interests

Sample CV

CURRICULUM VITAE

PERSONAL DETAILS

NAME	Stephen Loughran
ADDRESS	Riverside House, Bridge Street, Cork Road, Bandon, Co. Cork
TELEPHONE	(023) 496803
MOBILE	086 7724391
E-MAIL	sloughran@hotmail.com
DATE OF BIRTH	16 July 1982

EDUCATION

1994–2000	Bandon Comprehensive School, Bandon
2000–02	Drumlinn College of Further Education
	FETAC Course in Web-Design
	Modules: Graphic Design, Computer Applications,
	Desktop Publishing, Marketing, Communications,
	Computer Theory, Work Placement, Web Theory,
	HTML Programming, Business Law.

QUALIFICATIONS

1997	Junior Certificate

2000	Leaving Certificate		
	SUBJECT	LEVEL	GRADE
	Irish	O	C
	English	H	C
	Mathematics	O	C
	History	H	B
	Biology	O	D
	French	H	D
	Art	H	D

2002	FETAC Certificate in Web Design Level 2 (Merit)

WORK EXPERIENCE

1997-99   Supervalu, Bandon: Storehouse assistant

1999-2000   The Hanging Judge, Bandon: Barman

2000-02   E-Zee Internet Services and Web Design, Cork: Assistant Web Designer.

HONORARY POSITIONS

1998   School Chess Champion

2000   School Prefect

2000-01   Chairman Student Council, Drumlinn College

INTERESTS

Swimming

Photography

Chess

REFEREES

GERARD DALTON

Manager

E-Zee Internet Services and Web Design

22 Main Street

Cork

RICHARD D'ARCY

Web Design Course Co-ordinator

Drumlinn College of Further Education

Drumlinn

Co. Monaghan

 # Memorandum

A memo is a short message used internally in organisations to convey or request information, to confirm spoken communication or to give instructions. The word comes form the Latin for 'something to be remembered'. It can often be quite informal in style, depending on the organisation. Since a memo is such a short document, A5 paper is normally used, although A4 is also acceptable. As in business letters a reference number/initial can be used, Cc indicates copies sent to other parties and Enc means there is an accompanying note or document. A memo may be typed or hand-written, and deals with just one item of business.

Many companies have their own standardised memo forms. There are a variety of items that may be included on a memo but generally the following are the most important:

The sender, the recipient, the date and the subject matter. Open punctuation and fully blocked style is usual today.

Sample Memo

MEMORANDUM

TO   All Staff

FROM   P. Jacob

DATE   10 August 2002

REF   PJ/SB

SUBJECT   New Computer Software

The new computer software has just been installed. As most staff members will be unfamiliar with its operation, I would suggest a demonstration for an hour on 15 Thursday at 10.30 a.m. in the main office. Des Griffin has kindly volunteered to show us how to use it.

Assessment Activities

1. You are working in a department store. Write a memo to your colleagues informing them about your Christmas Social including dates, times, venue and costs.
2. You are the manager of a company/organisation (select appropriate vocational area). Write a memo to your staff informing them of some new equipment that has been installed, with instructions for use/suggestion for a demonstration at a particular time and place.
3. You are the manager of a company/organisation (select appropriate vocational area). Write a memo to your staff informing them that some members are taking lunch breaks that extend beyond the one hour limit. Explain reasons why there is a one hour lunch break and how extended breaks might adversely affect business.
4. You are the manager of a company/organisation (select appropriate vocational area). Write a memo to your staff informing them about the importance of punctuality in the workplace, as some members have been arriving late in the mornings and leaving early in the evenings.

Confusing Words

In each of the following sentences, select the correct word, decide what the other word means and put it into another sentence (it may have more than one meaning):

1. The patient is suffering from minor/miner injuries to the leg and back.
2. He worked as a naval/navel officer on board a coastal patrol boat.
3. Wash your face in the morning due/dew on the first of May and you'll remain forever young and beautiful.
4. I have a write/right to know.
5. I hope we've/weave packed enough clothes for this trip.
6. At 10.30 we were already/all ready to leave.
7. The president sought the council/counsel of his chief ministers.
8. The arrival of the president is eminent/imminent.

Chapter 7 Reports

Like other forms of written communication, reports vary in length, content, format and style depending on the purpose for which they are intended. Essentially a report is a presentation of facts following an investigation or examination. Reports may be written or presented orally. Many professions, such as the Gardaí, the medical profession, the civil service and of course the teaching profession require reports to be written regularly.

Types of Report

Routine Reports

These are submitted routinely, are brief and often written on specially provided forms. Doctors' reports on patients and teachers' reports on students are two examples.

Special Reports

Special reports are normally carried out and written for a specific purpose, for example, a fire officer may be called in to a firm to investigate the necessary improvements needed so that a building meets the requirements of the fire department. These reports are usually short and may be approximately 500-1000 words in length. Some reports may be so brief that they take the form of a memo.

Long Reports

As the name suggests, these are lengthy documents often taking the form of a book. Large corporations and State bodies will commission long reports and they may take many months to prepare. The Beef Tribunal Report and The Hamilton Report are recent Irish examples of these.

Reports may also be categorised as *formal* or *informal*.

Short Report

We will look at the short formal report here as it is the most likely type of report we will come across in our working lives. We may also be required to write such a report as a college assignment.

 # The short report follows a conventional structure

Title
Example:
'Report on Fire Safety at Dún Laoghaire Music Centre.'

Terms of Reference
This refers to the purpose, subject and limits of the report. If the report is required to make recommendations, they will be stated here with the name of the commissioning body or agent.

Example:

'As requested by the management, to investigate the adequacy of the fire safety procedures and facilities at the centre and to make any necessary recommendations.'

The terms of reference are always put in quotation marks.

Method of Procedure
The method of investigation is indicated here. This will include what kind of research was done and how it was carried out. The research may include the following:

- Surveys
- Interviews
- Questionnaires
- Observations
- Experiments
- Secondary research from books, magazines, newspapers, libraries, Internet etc.
  (See Chapter 8, Research Assignment)

Findings
The results of the investigation are called the findings and they make up the main body of the report. These must be presented in a clear, logical, objective and impersonal style. The use of headings, sub-headings and/or a numbering system will make it easier to refer to particular points in the report in any future discussion.

Conclusions

These must be based on the findings. They should be printed in descending order of importance and, without bias, should be the author's informed opinion.

Recommendations

Also presented in descending order of importance, recommendations are practical suggestions by the author based upon the findings and conclusions.

Signature and Date

The author signs the report and dates it.

Remember

When writing a report remember:

- The purpose of the report – is it to provide information, recommendations, analysis of facts?
- Who is going to read it?
- What does the reader already know about the subject?
- How much detail is required?
- Use language that is impersonal and objective. Use the passive voice - 'it is recommended that…' as opposed to the active voice – 'I recommend that…'
- Be clear and concise.
- Always draft, redraft, edit and proofread. Ideally ask someone else to proofread your work.
- Use graphs and charts for results of statistical information. (See Chapter 11, Visual Communication)
- Use images, illustrations and clip art to add interest (only if they are relevant).
- Keep it accurate and factual.

Sample of a Special Formal Report (Short)

Report on Fire Safety at Dún Laoghaire Music Centre

Terms of Reference
'As requested by the management, to investigate the adequacy of the fire safety procedures and facilities at the centre and to make any necessary recommendations.'

Method of Procedure
The local fire officer was contacted and requested to make a visit to the centre for a consultation with the centre's Health and Safety Officer.

He made a thorough inspection of the building to check fire-fighting equipment, alarm system, fire exits, notices and procedures for fire drills and emergency evacuation, and reported to the Health and Safety Officer.

Members of staff were asked if they knew how to operate the different types of fire extinguisher, how to recognise them and if they were well acquainted with the evacuation procedures already in place.

Findings
Present position

There are five fire exits in the centre. Each room in the centre is within walking distance of a fire exit.

The alarm system is functioning properly.

Fire notices in rooms are old and worn, and difficult to read clearly.

No fire drill has taken place in the past two years.

There are three fire hoses, and seven fire extinguishers in the building, three water, two dry chemical and two Carbon Dioxide (CO_2) extinguishers. None had been tested in the past four years. One of the water and one of the dry chemical extinguishers were faulty and one of the CO_2 extinguishers was almost empty. The rest of the extinguishers were in order.

Staff members do not know the difference in appearance between the three types of fire extinguisher in the college, nor their uses for different classes of fire.

Conclusions
No one is up-to-date with the emergency evacuation procedures. Staff are not sure which exits correspond to the different rooms.

It is not known if all the fire fighting equipment is in full working order.
Members of staff do not know how to use the various types of fire fighting equipment.

Recommendations
Devise new procedures for fire prevention and emergency evacuation.

Design new fire notices for each room indicating which exit is to be used from each room.

Invite the local fire officer to the centre to:

Talk to all staff about the various uses of each type of fire extinguisher, and to give a demonstration of each.

Advise on the upgrading and purchasing of new fire fighting equipment.

Purchase new fire-fighting equipment.

Appoint a member of staff to be Fire Officer, in charge of fire prevention and safety and to maintain equipment and notices.

Theresa McArdle: _____

Date: 20 February 2003

Students may be required to write a report as an assignment requiring careful research and planning. The guidelines on report writing here are fairly basic so the next chapter deals with the preparation and production of a research assignment. The style of the report might depend on individual course requirements so read through the next chapter before tackling a report as an assignment.

Assessment Activity

Write a report on your place of work experience. Here are some suggested guidelines for topics:

1. The history and background of the organisation/company/business
2. The ownership and management
3. Identification of the key personnel, their duties and responsibilities
4. A full description of the organisation/company/business, its buildings, facilities, resources, access, security, maintenance, daily routine, e.g opening and closing times
5. The impact of the organisation/company/business on the local community, economy, culture, environment etc.
6. A survey of the clients and customers, their use of the facilities and how they rate them etc.
7. A SWOT analysis, i.e. a list of strengths, weaknesses, opportunities and threats
8. Conclusions and recommendations as to any improvements that would enhance the organisation/company/business

Chapter Review

1. What is the purpose of a report?
2. Briefly explain the meaning of:
   (a) Terms of reference   (b) Method of procedure
   (c) Findings   (d) Conclusion   (e) Recommendations

Confusing Words

In each of the following sentences, select the correct word, decide what the other word means and put it into another sentence (it may have more than one meaning):

1. I'm going to give him a peace/piece of my mind.
2. The king's rain/rein/reign lasted for only two years.
3. Since the demise of traditional religious values society has become amoral/immoral.
4. The speeding juggernaut collided with a stationary/stationery car at the side of the road.
5. I wonder weather/whether the weather/whether will get any better.
6. We did an in debt/in depth study of the situation and then wrote a report.
7. I think I've past/passed all my exams.
8. I'm off to the club to practise/practice my moves.
9. My car is bigger then/than your car.

Chapter 8 Research Assignment

Report, assignment or project, are various words used to describe written work based upon some research carried out. The preparation and production of an assignment for a further education course will certainly require several communication skills such as reading, making enquiries, interviewing and of course writing. In most cases a specific brief will be given by the course tutor, including the format and length of the assignment, and a deadline.

 ## Preparation

First of all, make a note of your deadline. If you miss the deadline, your assignment may not be marked. Work out how much time you have in which to write the assignment, bearing in mind you may need a week or two at the end to proofread, polish and word process. There are always fiddly extras in the closing stages that we forget such as numbering pages, putting together a table of contents, a cover page and the bibliography. These are all dealt with further on in this section. It is useful to draw up a plan so you have an idea of when you will do the research and when you will do the actual writing. Choose specific times during the week to set aside for regular 'assignment time'. Part of the job is being organised and if you do a little every week for six to eight weeks, you will be more successful than if you cram it all into one or two weeks at the end.

Choosing a Topic

If you have the option of choosing a topic, then it is vital that you decide on something that:
1. Interests you – especially if you are going to be spending a month or two working on it.
2. Is easy to research – it is pointless doing an assignment on an obscure topic like 'The Habitats of Mongolian Wild Fowl', that will be impossible to research.

Begin with a brainstorming session. Write down everything you already know about the subject, followed by what you think you need to find out. You may get a brief from your tutor with instructions about how to research or specific details that you must include in your research. Next you need to think about where and how you will get your information.

Research

You cannot write an assignment based purely on what you already know, or from class notes and handouts. You have to go and do some thorough research yourself. The strength or weakness of an assignment often rests upon how much research has been done, how it has been carried out and how it is presented. Extensive and relevant research will yield a good result.

There are two types of research:
1. Primary Research – information that is gathered firsthand by means of surveys, interviews, questionnaires, observation, experiments and testing.
2. Secondary Research – Information that is gathered from material that has already been produced by someone else, e.g. books, brochures, leaflets, magazines, newspapers, the Internet, reports and other research papers.

Primary Research

Telephone Directory

If we know the name of an organisation that can provide us with first hand information, the telephone directory is an obvious starting point. It contains the State Directory at the beginning, which lists government services and departments, local authorities and health boards. A list of businesses in the second half of the directory could also prove useful. Many organisations will gladly oblige by sending out leaflets and information packs if necessary. The directory has addresses as well as telephone numbers, so a letter followed by a phone call is often the best way to request information.

Questionnaire

A questionnaire is a common method of primary research and is useful for obtaining facts and figures that can be used for statistical analysis. When designing a questionnaire consider the following:

1. What exact information is required?
2. Who will supply the information?
3. Will the respondents understand the questions and be able to answer them?
4. Are the questions clear and unambiguous?
5. In what sequence should the questions be arranged?
6. Is the layout clear?
7. How will the results be formulated, i.e. in tables, charts, graphs etc.?

A poorly designed questionnaire will yield poor results. It should be as user friendly as possible and should be tested on a few people, friends, family or classmates, before undertaking the survey proper.

Layout of the Questionnaire

1. Title of survey
2. Some factual questions
3. More complicated, multiple-choice questions
4. Open-ended questions
5. Identification questions (age, gender, nationality etc.)

Types of Question

Dichotomous questions require an answer of either yes or no. Boxes may be used for the respondent to tick. Tick boxes like these are very user-friendly, as respondents don't have to spend too much time thinking or writing.

Example:

Do you drive a car? Yes ❑   No ❑

Multiple-choice questions supply a number of possible answers from which the respondent can choose. Leave a space for 'other' in case there is an option you haven't considered.

Example:

Do you travel to work:

by bus   ❑
by car   ❑
by train ❑
by bike   ❑
on foot   ❑
other (please specify) _____

Open-ended questions give the respondent the option of giving a more lengthy and detailed reply, so remember to leave a few lines before the next question.

Example:

What improvements would you like to see? _____

_____

_____

Scaling questions ask the respondent to rate something. There are three types of scale:

1. The *Likert Scale* asks the respondent to agree or disagree with something.

   Example:

   The Internet is a useful means of research.

Strongly agree	Agree	Neither agree nor disagree	Disagree	Strongly disagree

2. The *Semantic-differential* presents the respondent with a scale of two opposing adjectives, and he indicates with a mark on that scale his attitude toward a specific issue or product.

   Example:

   Monkstown Leisure Centre is:

   Well maintained ————————————————————— Poorly maintained

   A mark on the very left means he thinks it is very well maintained and on the very right, poorly maintained. A mark in the middle indicates average.

3. The *Staple Scale* consists of one adjective in the middle of a numbered scale.

   Example:

   Do you think the staff in the centre are:

-5	-4	-3	-2	-1	friendly	+1	+2	+3	+4	+5
-5	-4	-3	-2	-1	helpful	+1	+2	+3	+4	+5
-5	-4	-3	-2	-1	efficient	+1	+2	+3	+4	+5

Analysis of the Results

When the questionnaires have been completed by the required number of respondents (aim for between twenty and thirty), they need to be objectively analysed and the details tabulated, in other words put into a table, chart or diagram. (See chapter 12, Visual Production)

Interviews

If you decide to interview someone, consider how you will conduct the interview. If you are going to meet the person face-to-face you should contact her by email, letter or by telephone, to request and set up a meeting. It is useful to follow up an email or letter with a phone call. It is also possible to conduct an interview over the telephone. Whichever way you decide to proceed, you need to be prepared. The seven questions at the start of the questionnaire section will apply here also. It is important to know exactly what information you are looking for.

Always prepare a list of questions before the interview. If you arrive ill-prepared you will appear unprofessional and the interview will take longer. Some people might get annoyed if you are unprepared, as they will feel their time is being wasted. If well prepared, you can tell an interviewee how long the interview might take. It is worth considering that they may find the work you are doing useful and therefore a professional approach on your part will increase their co-operation.

Decide how you will include the information from your interview into the main body of your assignment. You might quote the interviewee in relevant sections (see quotations below), or refer to points made by her (see references below). Avoid simply reproducing the interview at the end.

Observation

This means observing people, activities, organisations, events, and patterns of behaviour, objects etc. and making careful notes on your observations. For example, if you are researching the waste collection in your local community, you might observe what day and time the bin lorry arrives each week to remove rubbish and you can note down this information.

Experiments and Testing

Scientific experimenting and testing needs to be carefully monitored, and as with observation, notes must be made of each stage of an experiment.

Secondary Research
Encyclopaedia/Encarta

An encyclopaedia is useful for getting general information on a topic, and Encarta is Microsoft's encyclopaedia on CD-Rom (Compact Disc Read-only memory). A free online encyclopaedia is available at: *www.encyclopedia.com*

Libraries

Most towns have a good public library and membership is usually free. You might need to show evidence of address, such as an electricity bill or if under 18, a parent or guardian must act as guarantor. Many of us tend to forget about libraries these days as the Internet can provide much of our information requirements. However, finding one good book on our assignment topic can be far more useful and practical than spending many frustrating hours, surfing the Web and finding nothing that is relevant. If a library doesn't have exactly what you need the staff will often order a book for you. The inter-library loan system operates in some areas that might have more than one library, so if your local one doesn't have what you want they can check to see if another one nearby has it. A library might also have computer catalogues, daily newspapers and magazines, a photocopying service, computer facilities, Internet access, CDs, cassettes and CD-ROMS containing information that can be viewed on a computer. If you are unable to locate something, don't be afraid to ask for assistance.

IPA Yearbook

The Institute of Public Administration Yearbook contains information on most companies and organisations in Ireland and is usually available for reference in all public libraries.

Central Statistics Office

The Central Statistics Office is a Government agency that provides statistics on social and economic trends in Ireland. They also have a useful website: *www.cso.ie*

Internet/World Wide Web

If you are a frequent surfer of the Internet you know how useful it can be. It can also be very frustrating if you are unfamiliar with it and cannot find what you're looking for. Once we know how to conduct an effective search on the web, it can be an invaluable research tool. Academic research, after all, was one of the original purposes of the Internet. For more detailed information on searching the Internet see chapter 21.

Newspapers, Magazines, Journals

It is often possible to find information from these types of publication, depending on the kind of assignment we are researching. There are many specialist magazines that might be useful. Many newspapers are available online, with an archive facility for searching back issues, although we generally can't go back much further than the early 90s. This facility depends on the newspaper.

Reports, Brochures and Leaflets

Many organisations will publish their own annual report, (containing information on personnel, policy and finances); publicity brochures and leaflets can provide some basic facts.

All four types of reading come into play when conducting secondary research for an assignment. We scan to locate specific details that we need, skim to get an overview of the material, read at normal pace for general understanding and close read for more difficult material.

When you find a textbook, which you think you might be interested in there are several parts to skim:
- Title
- Contents
- Summary/Conclusion
- Headings/sub-headings
- Illustration and captions

These will give you a broad overview of what the book is about. If there is specific information you require, scan the index, if there is one, at the back to see if it is there. A bibliography (see below) can also be useful for further research.

As soon as you start to use written material for research it is crucial to record the following:
- Title
- Author(s)

- Date of publication
- Publisher
- Place of publication

For information retrieved from the Internet, record the title of the page or article, author if there is one and the URL or address. This information will be included in your bibliography (see below).

Format

An assignment is a formal, functional piece of writing, and uses conventional types of structure and layout. Assignments will vary in length – anything from 200 to 2000 words. Many tutors will give you their own guidelines on how to use the appropriate format. If you are writing a report, see chapter 7 for its own specific format. The following guidelines are suited to assignments of approximately 500 words or more.

Structure
Title/Cover Page
This should include a title and your name. A suitable visual, a coloured font and a page border can all enhance the presentation. Don't use fonts that are illegible or too decorative. Remember it is a formal document.

Contents Page
A list of your section/chapter headings followed by their page numbers.

Aim
The aim should state the purpose of the assignment, what type of research was used and how it was carried out. This need only be a short paragraph. In a report format this is called Terms of Reference (see Chapter 7).

Introduction
The purpose of an introduction is to introduce the reader to the assignment. Consider how much the reader may or may not already know about the subject. It could be three to four paragraphs long, but certainly no longer than a page. Begin with a general introduction to the subject stating why it is important, relevant or interesting and gradually become more specific towards the end. For example, if your subject is on e-commerce in Ireland, begin with some general background information about e-commerce, its origins, history to date, and then go on to explain why it is important in today's business world, and finally outline the current situation in Ireland. An introduction should be an overview, telling the reader what to expect in the main body. Don't include too many details.

Main Body

This will be divided into chapters or sections that will vary in length depending on the size of the work. Each section should start on a new page with a heading at the top, centred and in bold and/or underlined. Make sure all headings are of a consistent style. Sub-headings should be smaller, placed on the left-hand margin, and can also be in bold and/or underlined.

The following can be used for lists of sub-headings or other items.

1. Numbering, i.e. 1., 2.
2. Lettering, i.e. (a), (b)
3. Bullet points, i.e. •

Conclusion

The conclusion should contain:

1. An analysis, examining the main points of the contents or findings
2. Evidence of critical thinking, that is, giving an *informed* opinion based on facts acquired from the research
3. Recommendations of what actions need to be taken
4. An indication of the possible future outcome of an organisation or situation
5. A reference back to the aim, stating if and how successfully it was achieved

   It should be approximately two to three paragraphs in length.

Bibliography

See below for details.

Appendix

This contains any additional information such as research notes, copies of letters sent and received, copy of a questionnaire, if one was used and a detailed record of telephone calls made etc.

Language and Style

The style of a written assignment should be clear, impersonal and objective. Avoid using the first and second person, e.g. 'I' 'me' 'my', 'you' and 'your'. So instead of 'The aim of my assignment is...' write 'The aim of this assignment is...'. Use the passive voice. So instead of, 'I carried out a survey...' write 'A survey was carried out...'

Objectivity means your writing is unbiased and supported by evidence obtained through sound research, not from what you might just feel, think or believe. Avoid making statements and comments that aren't based on your research. There should be evidence of original thinking, so don't be afraid to include some ideas of your own, as long as they are relevant and based on the research you've carried out.

References

An assignment should be written in your own words. Under no circumstances should passages of text be copied, word for word, from other sources, and passed off as your own work. This is called plagiarism, and is in breach of the copyright laws. It needs to show evidence of the research carried out and this is done by including references to other works and written material. Here are the main types of referencing:

Quotations

Quotations must be taken from the text word for word. Short quotations should be placed within quotation marks and be followed with the author's surname, year of publication and page number.

Example:

'You can't get away from the Internet these days.' (Butler, 2000, p. 1)

This means the quotation is taken from a book by someone by the name of Butler, published in the year 2000, and is taken from page 1. The reader can then refer to the bibliography and check the details of the book.

Long quotations (three lines or more) are separated from the rest of the text and indented.

Example:

> You can't get away from the Internet these days. Everywhere you go, you see references to web sites, e-mail addresses, e-commerce. When you meet old friends, they won't ask for your address or phone number, they'll ask you for your e-mail address. Everybody...has a different opinion of the Internet, what it is and what it means to them.
> (Butler, 2000: 1)

Words omitted from a quoted piece are indicated by an *ellipsis* (...). This is useful if a passage contains words in the middle that are irrelevant, and you want to leave them out.

Quotations from an interview should be presented the same way, but followed in brackets by the name of the interviewee and the word 'interview' and if possible the date the interview took place.

A *citation* is a reference to another author's work, which must include the year of publication.

Example:

Butler (2000) states that the Internet is unavoidable these days.

Again, the reader can then check in the bibliography for books by Butler.

 # Bibliography

A bibliography is a list of all the written sources of information used for research. It should go at the end of the main body of the project, after the conclusion, before the appendix. Essentially its purpose is twofold:

1. To show that you have done some research and so that the assessor can check the sources of that research if need be

2. To acknowledge the authors of written works you have used. This is common courtesy and also shows you haven't plagiarised their work

Head the page with the word 'Bibliography', in a style and font consistent with the rest of the assignment. Works are listed in alphabetical order of author's surname and are not numbered. Different source types require different kinds of entries, but all should be listed together regardless of whether the information is from a book, video, Internet, newspaper etc.

Books

Surname of author(s), first name(s)/initial(s), year of publication, *title* (underlined or in italics), publisher, place of publication. Note commas separating each item.

Butler, R., 2000, *The Internet Demystified*, Oak Tree Press, Dublin.

Newspapers, magazines, journals

Author(s), year of publication, 'title of article' (in inverted commas), *title of journal*, date/month/volume/issue number, page number(s).

Holt, E., 2000, 'Who's watching the media?' *The Irish Times – Weekend*, 2 December 2000, p. 6

Encyclopaedias

Title, year of publication, publisher, place of publication, volume number, page number(s).

Philip's Concise Encyclopedia, 1997, George Philip Ltd., London, p.132.

Pamphlets, brochures, leaflets

Title, year of publication, publisher, place of publication.

Ireland's Environment, Take Action Now!, 2000, Environmental Protection Agency, Wexford.

Edited Works (books with a selection of essays by different authors)

Author(s), year of publication, 'title of essay/chapter', In name of editor(s), (Ed(s).) *title of publication*, publisher, place of publication.

Fiske, J., 1991, 'Postmodernism and Television', In Curran, J. and Gurevitch, M. (Eds.) *Mass Media and Society*, Edward Arnold, London.

CD-ROMs

Title, [CD-ROM], year of publication, publisher, place of publication.

Encarta, [CD-ROM], 2001, Microsoft, USA.

Video

Title, [Video], year of publication, publisher, place of publication.

Body Language, [Video], 2001, Simply Communication, Galway.

Internet

Author, year of publication, *title*, [Online], Internet address, date of access.

Floyd, G., McKay, J., 2001, *Writing a Bibliography* (Harvard System), [Online], *http://www.dicksonc.act.edu.au/Library/bibliog.html*, 15 July 2001.

Email

Author(s), year of publication, *Title/subject*, [Personal email], date of access.

Brophy, J., 2001, *Punctuation*, [Personal email], 14 April.

Interviews

Name of interviewee, year of interview, position of interviewee, [Interview], date of interview.

McLelland, S., 2002, Manager of Leitrim Tourist Office, [Interview], 14 November.

 # Chapter Review

1. Give a brief explanation of primary and secondary research.
2. What are the main sources of information for secondary research?
3. What is the purpose of a bibliography?

Confusing Words

In each of the following sentences, select the correct word, decide what the other word means and put it into another sentence (it may have more than one meaning):

1. The mountaineers began their decent/descent.
2. She thought/taught English as a foreign language in Spain for a year.
3. The new target market was given the hard sell/cell.
4. We have to be discrete/discreet about what we say.
5. The government has an appalling waist/waste management policy.
6. How did you fair/fare in your last position?
7. They waited for the storm to seas/sees/cease before setting out on their journey.
8. He was the sole/soul survivor of the plane crash.

Topics Covered

Punctuation

Confusing Words

Grammar Basics

GLASBERGEN

"If we eliminate vowels and punctuation from all corporate communications, we can save $400 a year on ink and toner."

Punctuation

Without punctuation, written language would make little sense. Look at the following:

i know when he exclaimed well do it this evening thats settled then she said the party was a great success

'I know when!' he exclaimed. 'We'll do it this evening.'
'That's settled then,' she said.
The party was a great success.

This is why we punctuate written communication, so that the reader understands clearly and without ambiguity the meaning of the written word. Writing cannot convey meaning like speaking does – with tone of voice, volume, speed etc. so punctuation is our best way of doing this. Computer technology can help with automatic checks and predictive writing, but these tools can cause our writing skills to become rusty if we become too dependent upon them. So we still need to know the basics in order to produce good meaningful pieces of writing.

Capital Letters

The capital letter is used:

- To begin all sentences including direct speech: **H**e said, '**H**ello.'
- For proper nouns i.e. names of people, countries, organisations, buildings, geographical features, historical events and festivals: **J**im, **E**stonia, **G**reenpeace, the **T**aj **M**ahal, the **A**mazon, the **T**reaty of **V**ersailles, the **E**dinburgh **F**ringe **F**estival.
- For proper adjectives i.e. derived from proper nouns: **F**rench, **T**arantinoesque
- For the personal pronoun '**I**'
- For acronyms: **AIDS, UNESCO**
- For well-known geographical regions, e.g. the **N**orth
- For titles of books, newspapers, magazines, television and radio programmes, plays, songs, poems, films, people (though conjunctions are not included, e.g. and, but, because etc., nor prepositions - of, in, by, beside, for, from etc., nor 'a' in the middle) '**T**he **W**izard of **O**z', '**R**omeo and **J**uliet'.
- For days of the week and for months, not for seasons of the year

Activity

Rewrite the following putting capital letters in where necessary:

paula worked at the bayview hotel as an assistant manager. she had studied hotel management at drumlinn college of further education. the hotel was situated just off the n16 to ballybrady, just south of mount lisslee. one spring day, the hotel was visited by a delegation from the european committee of health and safety officers. flying into a panic, paula called all the staff and said, 'now i want this place to look like a new pin.' when the echso delegation arrived, the president, a professor ingmar klugmann, who had a phd in musicology, said they weren't going to have an inspection but demanded to hear some traditional irish music. so, seán, the chef from the west, took out his tin whistle and played them his version of 'the fields of athenry'.

The Apostrophe (')

The apostrophe is used in nouns to indicate *possession* or *belonging*, e.g. Fred's cat. We usually add an apostrophe and an 's'.

Plurals with an 's'

For plurals that already have an 's', the apostrophe goes after the 's'.

Compare:

The cat's paws are black. (One cat)

The cats' paws are black. (More than one cat)

Plurals without an 's'

For plurals that don't have an 's', e.g. women, children, mice, we add an apostrophe and an 's':

The mouse's tail is brown.

The mice's tails are brown.

Basic Rule

The basic rule is:

- If there is an 's' at the end of the word already, the apostrophe goes after it and no further 's' is added.
- If there is no 's', add an apostrophe and an 's'.
- For nouns that end in an 's', add an apostrophe and an 's':
  - The boss's office.
  - Mr Burns's nose.
  - Bridget Jones's Diary.
- For longer names with the accent on the first syllable, both forms are acceptable:
  - Nicholas' bicycle.
  - Nicholas's bicycle.
- For ancient classical names ending in 's', add an apostrophe:
  - Herodotus' book.
  - Jesus' and Jesus's are both acceptable.

Activity

Change the following phrases and add apostrophes where required:

e.g. 'The cage of the hamster' becomes 'The hamster's cage'.

1. The assignments of the students
2. The plays of Shakespeare
3. The feet of Moses
4. The organ works of Bach
5. The toys of the children
6. The bones of the dog
7. The Green of St Stephen
8. The wool of the lambs
9. The Square of St Thomas
10. The surface of Mars

Note the Expressions:
- A fortnight's holiday
- Two weeks' holiday
- One week's time
- One pound's worth
- Five pounds' worth
- For God's sake
- For goodness' sake

Also:
- She went to the dentist's.
- We are off to the butcher's.
    In each case a word has been left out - surgery and shop.

Abbreviations

The apostrophe is used in abbreviations to indicate that a letter has been left out, e.g. I'm = I am, doesn't = does not, he'll = he will.

Activity
Abbreviate the following:
1. could not
2. they are
3. shall not
4. we have
5. who will
6. she is
7. it has
8. who would

The Apostrophe is Not Used
- For plurals such as 'No dog's allowed' and 'Fish and Chip's'. These are both wrong and should be 'No dogs' and 'Fish and Chips'
- Plurals of numbers/years: the 1960s
- Plurals of abbreviations: PCs, OAPs, B&Bs
- Possessive Pronouns: hers, its, ours, yours, theirs.

Confusables

its = belonging to it

it's = it is/it has.

whose: The man whose wife sang at the opera.

who's = who is/who has: Who's on the phone?

Activity

Insert apostrophes into the following sentences:

1. We went for a fortnights holiday to Donegal.
2. Its been raining all day and Im soaked.
3. Theres a message in your mail box, isnt there?
4. Its not mine its hers.
5. For heavens sake, I dont care whos here.
6. Were going away on St Stephens Day.
7. Heres Dereks jacket. Its filthy.
8. Ill get an hours work done before the film.

Hyphen (-)

The hyphen:

1. Joins words to make new words, e.g. hard-working, sister-in-law, film-maker, pin-stripe, state-of-the-art, ten-year-old.
2. Divides a word that won't fit at the end of a line, e.g. dis-
   connected. Of course, when word processing this is unnecessary as the words are fitted neatly into the page automatically.

Dash (–)

The dash separates:

1. Words and phrases in the middle of a sentence, e.g
   - The band – the best in the country – has just embarked on a world tour.
   - Two young men – both beginners – joined the course yesterday.
2. Words or phrases added on to the end of sentences, e.g.
   - The street has a lively atmosphere – just what we were looking for.
   - We drove down the coastline – one of the most beautiful I'd ever seen.

The dash is often regarded as slightly informal. The same key is used for both a hyphen and a dash on the keyboard. When word-processing put a space either side for a dash.

Activity

The following passage needs six hyphens and seven dashes:

My sister in law came to stay for the weekend she didn't even ring to warn us! Her husband my brother Harry is a long legged evil looking man he even scares the dog. We watched the semi final on television and then were about to have a big feed of pasta my favourite when we noticed the sell by date on the packet two weeks old!

Colon (:)

The colon:

1. Indicates that something is following on from the previous phrase or sentence, e.g.
   You know what will happen if you miss the deadline: you'll fail the assignment.
2. Introduces a series or list:
   Here's what I'm having: soup, lasagne, a side salad, ice cream and coffee.
3. Introduces a quotation:
   As Bob Dylan said: 'Keep a good head and always carry a light bulb.'

Semi-colon (;)

The semi-colon:

1. Is used to separate two parts of a sentence which are too closely connected to be separated by a full stop, e.g.
   • I love apples; granny smiths are my favourite.
   • To lose one parent is unfortunate; to lose both is carelessness.
   • She was delighted; I was delirious.
   These could be written as separate sentences.
2. Can sometimes be replaced with 'but'.
3. Can also be used for a list in which the items are lengthy:
   John's travels took him far and wide: a week by the sea on a beautiful Greek island; a month exploring the rugged Turkish coastline; three weeks travelling south through the scorched landscape of the Middle East; and finally a month in Egypt exploring the ancient archaeological wonders.

Activity

Put a colon or semi-colon into the following sentences:
1. Out came the sun off came the shirts.
2. We'll need the following a hammer, nails, wood and paint.
3. Remember the proverb many hands make light work.
4. Here's the suspect's description 6'2" brown hair, brown eyes and a moustache.
5. The speaker began 'Good evening, Ladies and Gentlemen.'
6. Luxembourg is a small country France is a large one.

Full Stop, Question Mark, Exclamation Mark

The full stop is used:

1. At the end of sentences, normally followed by a capital letter to begin the next sentence

2. After initials: W.B. Yeats

3. After abbreviations: 25 Dec.

There is no full stop in a sequence of capitals - AIDS, UN, etc.

A sequence of three full stops, called *an ellipsis*, means an omission of a section of text: Everyone… seems to have used the Internet these days.

A *question mark* is used after questions instead of a full stop and is followed by a capital letter. It is not used after indirect questions.

An *exclamation mark* is used instead of a full stop after exclamations, which usually express some strong feeling, emphasis or humour.

Activity

Put a full stop, question mark or exclamation mark after each of the following sentences:

1. I don't know whether she's in or not
2. Do we know if there is alien life in the Universe
3. Help
4. I wonder if I could borrow your hammer
5. He told me why he was late
6. Don't you dare
7. How far do we have to travel
8. What a great idea

The Comma (,)

The following sentences can be very confusing without commas:

1. The discussion over the game continued.
2. The student thought the teacher was going to do very well.
3. The tiger having eaten the children walked on.
4. Granny has eaten Brian.

Where would you put them?

Separating Mark

The comma is a *separating mark*. It separates:

1. Phrases in a sentence where a natural pause occurs:
   • After the table was cleared, they began to play cards.

2. Descriptive phrases in the middle of a sentence, which are not essential to the meaning of the sentence:

- The novel, a murder mystery, will probably become a best seller.
- Mrs Malone, who was wearing a bright pink frock, poured the tea.

BUT

- The woman who was wearing a bright pink frock poured the tea.

(This is essential to the overall meaning.)

3. Items in a list of three or more items, but not before 'and':
   - We bought tea, milk, sugar and bread.
   - She climbed to the top of the wall, took out her binoculars, scanned the horizon and prepared for the worst.

Words that Introduce Direct Speech

- He said, 'You know, that's the worst sentence I've ever read.'
- 'You know,' he said, 'that's the worst sentence I've ever read.'
- 'You know, that's the worst sentence I've ever read,' he said.

Non-essential Additions to Sentences (including interjections like aha, oops, er, um etc.)

Well, I'm going to talk to you, about, like, the Drumlinn, aaah, Leisure Centre which, you know, is, situated near, I mean, not far from here, know what I mean like?

Question Tags (also non-essential additions)

- It's cold today, isn't it?
- You saw it, didn't you?

Vocatives (addressing a person or thing) and Salutations

- Mr President, I'd like to congratulate you.
- It's nice to see you again, Helen.
- Dear Sandra,

Sentence Adverbs (like 'however', 'nevertheless', 'meanwhile', 'finally', 'at last')

- There is, however, a good reason for studying this.
- Yes, I'd like that.
- No, I disagree.
- Of course, she'll never make the grade.

Participial (-ing) Phrases

Feeling energetic, he went for a run.

Parts of a Sentence to Avoid Confusion

- The discussion over, the game continued.
- The student, thought the teacher, was going to do very well.
- The tiger having eaten, the children walked on.
- Granny has eaten, Brian.

Wrong Uses of Comma

- I walked to the window, it was still open.
- At the end of the game, the players, were exhausted.
- Addresses: 12, Stephen Street.
- People, who live in glass houses, shouldn't throw stones.

Activity

Insert commas into the following sentences:

1. So Joe do you think we have a chance of winning?
2. The doctor a large friendly man prescribed some pills.
3. Singing at the top of his voice Steve prepared a splendid dinner.
4. Josephine meanwhile was reading the paper.
5. 'Don't you think' she enquired 'we should call the vet?'
6. When the builders arrived Jane was still having breakfast.
7. The train travelling at 120 mph had fourteen carriages.
8. According to the weatherman it should snow tonight.
9. I put on my coat picked up my things bade farewell and left the building.
10. You're finished now aren't you?

Inverted Commas/Quotation Marks (' ') ("")

Use either single ' ' or double " ". If using a quotation within a quotation use single for the first and double for the second:

She said, 'In the words of Roosevelt, "The only thing we have to fear is fear itself," and I must say I have to agree.'

Direct Speech

'You know,' she said, 'maybe we'll meet up again sometime.'

Punctuation marks, which belong to the quote, remain within the quotation marks. In a written passage a new speaker is indicated by a new paragraph.

Quotations

Quotations are used for what someone else said or wrote: As Descartes said, 'I think, therefore I am.'

Titles

Quotation marks indicate titles of poems, songs, articles in newspapers or magazines and short stories: 'The Lake Isle of Innisfree' is a favourite poem in Ireland.

Colloquialisms

Colloquialisms or words that have new or strange meanings can be indicated by the use of quotation marks: I popped into my 'chat-room' last night.

Activity

Insert quotation marks, if necessary, into the following sentences:
1. It's all right she said everything will be better in the morning.
2. What kind of a word is bodacious anyway he enquired.
3. What do you mean I'm a Babe she asked.
4. Give us your rendition of As Time Goes By.
5. Teachers to Strike yelled the headline across the front page.
6. In the words of Samuel Beckett: We are all born mad. Some remain so.

Brackets/Parentheses ()

These are used to enclose explanations, translations, definitions and added information to the text:

His philosophy was always *carpe diem* (seize the day).

(If an entire sentence is enclosed in brackets, the full stop must come within the final bracket.)

Activity

Put brackets into the following sentences:
1. The ship if you could call it that will sail at 10.30 pm
2. We sat in the shade it was too hot to do anything else drinking ice cold water.
3. The people who are really stressed these days not counting nurses are senior management.
4. The books both thrillers lay on his desk gathering dust.
5. She shouted after him, 'Ich liebe dich I love you,' but it was too late. He was gone.
6. This steady increase in temperature known as global warming is set to get worse over the coming century.

Confusing Words

Activity

Delete whichever words are incorrect from each of the following sentences:

1. There/their/they're is a group of men outside and there/their/they're carrying umbrellas under there/their/they're arms.
2. I've been/being at this bus stop for 45 minutes and I'm sick of been/being kept waiting.
3. Where/were/we're all going to Donegal, which is where/were/we're we where/were/we're last year for our holidays.
4. There are two/too/to gunslingers coming two/too/to this town. That is two/too/to two/too/to many.
5. It's/its been a long time since the union got it's/its way.

The following are often mistakenly written as two words, when in fact they should be one:
• thereby
• nearby
• whereas
• into
• altogether
• intact.

The following are often mistakenly written as single words, when in fact they should be two:
• as well
• in store
• a lot
• in fact
• in case.

Frequently Used Latin Abbreviations

• i.e. - id est (that is)
• e.g. - exempli gratia (for example)
• etc. - et cetera (and the rest)
• et al. - et alibi (and elsewhere), et alii/alia (and other people/things)

Beware of the following confusing phrases:
I could have been a contender. √
I could of been a contender. X

She should have stayed. √
She should of stayed. X
It would not have been possible. √
It would not of been possible. X

 # Grammar Basics

It would be impractical to cover the grammar of the English language in its entirety in this book, but a few basic points are worth making here.

Sentence

A sentence is often described as a set of words that has a complete meaning. It starts with a capital letter and ends with a full stop, question mark or exclamation mark. For a sentence to have complete meaning, it almost always has to have a two things:

1. Subject: who or what does the action, or about whom or what something is stated.
2. Predicate: refers to what the subject is or does

Example:

The student submitted the assignment.

This is a complete sentence, 'student' being the *subject*, and 'submitted' being the *predicate*; 'assignment' is what is called the *object.*

To make this sentence more interesting we can add:

1. An adjective:

The **brilliant** student submitted the assignment.

2. An adverb:

The brilliant student **hastily** submitted the assignment.

3. A preposition (and indirect object):

The brilliant student hastily submitted the assignment **to** the tutor.

4. A pronoun:

The brilliant student hastily submitted the assignment to **her** tutor.

Phrase

A phrase is a set of words that doesn't always have a complete meaning.

'to her tutor' is a phrase that doesn't mean anything on its own.

'The brilliant student' is a phrase that could mean something if for example it was a response to a question such as, 'Who submitted the assignment?'

Subject/Verb Agreement

The subject in a sentence must 'agree' with its verb. We cannot say 'The student submit the assignment' because the subject and verb do not agree. So both subject and verb should be either singular or plural and not a mixture.

Singular/Collective

These words take the singular: each, every, either, neither, any.

With collective nouns the singular or plural are both acceptable these days:

- The Government has/have raised taxes again.
- The audience was/were thrilled with the performance.

Activity

Correct the following sentences so that there is agreement between subject(s) and verb:

1. There is 450 students in the college.
2. Hector, together with his sister, Hattie, walk to school everyday.
3. The wages they pay is very low.
4. The driver and passenger is happy.
5. That herd of cattle have BSE.
6. Which one of you two are the manager?
7. All four of them has a PhD.
8. Each of them were studying for years.
9. 'The Simpsons' are my favourite TV programme.

Paragraph

A paragraph is a section of writing that usually deals with one specific topic. The writer states the topic in either the first or last sentence. In a handwritten piece the first sentence is indented. When word-processing, paragraphs are normally separated from each other by a line blank. Paragraphs give a piece of writing a tidy, ordered appearance and can make it easy for the reader to read.

Answers

Capital Letters

Paula worked at the Bayview Hotel as an assistant manager. She had studied Hotel Management at Drumlinn College of Further Education. The hotel was situated just off the N16 to Ballybrady, just south of Mount Lisslee. One spring day, the hotel was visited by a delegation from the European Committee of Health and Safety Officers. Flying into a panic, Paula called all the staff and said, 'Now I want this place to look like a new pin.' When the ECHSO delegation arrived, the President, a Professor Ingmar Klugmann, who had a PhD in Musicology, said they weren't going to have an inspection but demanded to hear some traditional Irish music. So, Seán, the chef from the West, took out his tin whistle and played them his version of 'The Fields of Athenry'.

Apostrophes

1. the students' assignments
2. Shakespeare's plays
3. Moses' feet
4. Bach's organ works
5. the children's toys
6. the dog's bones
7. St Stephen's Green
8. the lambs' wool
9. St Thomas's Square
10. Mars' surface

1. Couldn't
2. They're
3. Shan't
4. We've
5. Who'll
6. She's
7. It's
8. Who'd

1. We went for a fortnight's holiday to Donegal.
2. It's been raining all day and I'm soaked.
3. There's a message in your mail box, isn't there?
4. We've been waiting for ages.
5. For heaven's sake, I don't care who's here.
6. We're going away on St Stephen's Day.
7. Here's Derek's jacket. It's filthy.
8. I'll get an hour's work done before the film.

Six Hyphens and Seven Dashes

My sister-in-law came to stay for the weekend – she didn't even ring to warn us! Her husband – my brother Harry – is a long-legged evil-looking man – he even scares the dog. We watched the semi-final on television and then were about to have a big feed of pasta – my favourite – when we noticed the sell-by date on the packet – two weeks old!

Colon/Semi-Colon

1. Out came the sun; off came the shirts.
2. We'll need the following: a hammer, nails, wood and paint.
3. Remember the proverb: many hands make light work.

4. Here's the suspect's description: 6'2", brown hair, brown eyes and a moustache.

5. The speaker began: 'Good evening, Ladies and Gentlemen.'

6. Luxembourg is a small country; France is a large one.

Full Stop/Question Mark/Exclamation Mark

1. I don't know whether she's in or not.

2. Do we know if there is alien life in the Universe?

3. Help!

4. I wonder if I could borrow your hammer.

5. He told me why he was late.

6. Don't you dare!

7. How far do we have to travel?

8. What a great idea!

Commas

1. So Joe, do you think we have a chance of winning?

2. The doctor, a large friendly man, prescribed some pills.

3. Singing at the top of his voice, Steve prepared a splendid dinner.

4. Josephine, meanwhile, was reading the paper.

5. 'Don't you think,' she enquired, 'we should call the vet?'

6. When the builders arrived, Jane was still having breakfast.

7. The train, travelling at 120 mph, had fourteen carriages.

8. According to the weatherman, it should snow tonight.

9. I put on my coat, picked up my things, bade farewell and left the building.

10. You're finished now, aren't you?

Inverted Commas

1. 'It's all right,' she said, 'everything will be better in the morning.'

2. 'What kind of a word is "bodacious" anyway?' he enquired.

3. 'What do you mean I'm a "Babe"?' she asked.

4. Give us your rendition of 'As Time Goes By'.

5. 'Teachers to Strike' yelled the headline across the front page.

6. In the words of Samuel Beckett: 'We are all born mad. Some remain so.'

Brackets

1. The ship (if you could call it that) will sail at 10.30 pm.

2. We sat in the shade (it was too hot to do anything else) drinking ice-cold water.

3. The people who are really stressed these days (not counting nurses) are senior management.

4. The books (both thrillers) lay on his desk gathering dust.

5. She shouted after him, 'Ich liebe dich (I love you),' but it was too late. He was gone.

6. This steady increase in temperature (known as global warming) is set to get worse over the coming century.

Confusing Words

1. There is a group of men outside and they're carrying umbrellas under their arms.
2. I've been at this bus stop for 45 minutes and I'm sick of being kept waiting.
3. We're all going to Donegal, which is where we were last year for our holidays.
4. There are two gunslingers coming to this town. That is two too many.
5. It's been a long time since the union got its way.

Subject/Verb Agreement

1. There are 450 students in the college.
2. Hector, together with his sister, Hattie, walks to school everyday.
3. The wages they pay are very low.
4. The driver and passenger are happy.
5. That herd of cattle has BSE.
6. Which one of you two is the manager?
7. All four of them have a PhD.
8. Each of them was studying for years.
9. 'The Simpsons' is my favourite TV programme.

Confusing Words

In each of the following sentences, select the correct word, decide what the other word means and put it into another sentence (it may have more than one meaning):

1. We dropped into the off-licence/license to get some beer for the party.
2. Is this a licensed/licenced premises?
3. She decided to brake/break off/of their relationship.
4. I have an awful pain in my back. I hope I don't have a slipped disc/disk.
5. We saw a fantastic programme/program on television last night.
6. After all the Christmas eating and drinking, he was scared to way/weigh himself.
7. He called to say he'd be late due to a bored/board meeting.
8. Police are investigating an incidence/incident in a city centre shopping mall.

Part 3

Non-Verbal
Communication

Chapter 10 Non-Vebal Communication

Non-verbal communication means communicating without words. NVC probably accounts for over 80% of what we communicate, whereas the spoken word may be as little as 7%. A look can often reveal more accurately what we are thinking than words can. We are constantly communicating non-verbally, by the way we look, gesture, stand, sit, smile, frown, dress ourselves, wear our hair etc. This is why NVC is so important in any study of communication.

Let's look at a few general points about NVC before we examine the specific types.

1. NVC is ambiguous. There are always at least two potential meanings to any NVC, that of the sender and that of the receiver. It is not always possible to interpret the exact meaning of NVC as it depends on both the context and the people involved. We should not attempt to attach a fixed meaning to any one form of NVC in isolation from the other verbal and non-verbal messages that may be communicated with it.

2. NVC varies from culture to culture. What might be a friendly gesture in our culture, may be a serious insult in another, so be careful! The circle sign made with the thumb and forefinger means 'OK' to Irish, British, Americans and most Northern Europeans. In France it signifies 'zero' or 'worthless', in Japan, 'money', and in parts of the Mediterranean it is an obscene insult.

3. Most of our NVC is unconscious. We wave our hands about and gesticulate when talking excitedly; our face changes shape depending on our emotional state; we twitch, fidget, scratch, stretch, shift our posture hundreds of times every day without even noticing it.

4. We are much less aware of our NVC than our speech. If we become more conscious of how we communicate non-verbally, we can learn to control it and become better communicators.

5. NVC.
   - Supports speech – hand gestures reinforce, elaborate and emphasise what we say, e.g. 'I caught a fish *this* big!' 'He went *that* way.'
   - Modifies speech – we can say 'Don't do that' in an angry, pleading, firm, or light-hearted way.
   - Replaces speech – sign language.
   - Contradicts speech – 'Yes of course I'm fine!' she snapped, avoiding his gaze, and sighing heavily.

6. First impressions count. When we walk through that door for an interview, we are immediately being judged on our appearance, how we walk, shake hands and sit down. Jobs are often disproportionately offered on this basis.

7. Actions speak louder than words. If someone says he has time to talk to you, yet continues what he is doing: gathering his books, erasing the board and checking the register, do you believe his verbal or non-verbal message? Most people, when confronted by such contradictory signs, believe the non-verbal language. Since we are more in control of our words than our body language, most of us find it easier to lie verbally than non-verbally.

Fig. 10.1 The Beatles.

Compare these two photographs of the Beatles, one during their heyday, and the other shortly before their split. Discuss the differences in facial expression, physical proximity and contact.

Appearance

Fig. 10.2

Appearance says a lot about the type of person we are. Even if we are the kind of person who dresses 'down' so as not to attract unwanted attention, we are still communicating something about ourselves. We can change how we present ourselves by making alterations to our hair, facial hair, make-up, clothes, accessories, and by using jewellery, tattoos and body piercing. By doing this we can communicate messages about our:

- Personality – conservative, rebellious, artistic, individual, extrovert/introvert
- Occupation – some jobs have specific uniforms.
- Role – think of a few different roles you fill, e.g. at work, socialising (formal/informal, single/attached), at home, at an interview.
- Status – in some occupations higher status is illustrated by different clothing, e.g. the army, nursing, the church, expensive designer suits, etc.
- Nationality
- Gender
- Sexual orientation
- Interests and tastes
- Club membership

It is important to consider how we present ourselves in different situations. For example, for job interviews it is recommended that we dress formally. If we dress too formally for an occasion that is casual, we may look, and feel, out of place. Our appearance projects a certain image of ourselves, and other people will respond to that image. At work and in formal situations we tend to respond more positively to those who are well dressed, but not overdressed.

Consider the clothes you wear. Have you ever thought about the signals that you might be sending out with them? Do you wear them:

- For comfort/practical reasons
- Because they are fashionable
- To attract attention
- To blend in with the crowd
- To look 'cool'
- To appear sexy
- Because they are long lasting
- To look rebellious/different
- To be part of a clique
- Because they have a certain logo

What signals might the following be sending out:

- A male with long hair
- A female skinhead
- A male with short back and sides
- A Mohican
- Dreadlocks
- Pierced tongue
- Pierced eyebrow
- A male with a right earring only

Facial Expression

The most important, authentic and direct communication takes place face-to-face. The face is the best indicator of our feelings and it is only when we are face-to-face with someone that we really connect with him. Even though expressions like smiling and frowning are inborn, we learn how to respond facially to others through interaction with our parents, families and friends, so for example, we smile as a response to another's smile. There is a concern today that many children who don't receive enough parental interaction due to busy lifestyles, and spend much of their time using electronic games, lose out on healthy face-to-face contact. As a result they don't learn facial expression responses, and this can cause relationship problems in later life.

There are over 10,000 facial expressions caused by 44 facial muscles and two bones, the skull and the jaw. There are, however, seven primary expressions that promote a deep response in us: happiness, sadness, surprise, anger, fear, disgust and contempt.

The eyes and the mouth are the main communicators and they are the features we focus on mostly when we are looking at someone. Socrates said that the eyes are the windows of the soul and we can usually tell how someone really feels by looking at the eyes. A micro-expression in the eyebrows has been identified by experts as an indication of a lie. It is a minute and swift raising of the inner corners of the eyebrows creating a slight furrowed brow. When President Clinton denied the allegations of sexual relations with Monica Lewinsky, he made this action.

The mouth smiles, sneers, pouts, purses, grins, opens wide, shuts tightly etc. The ultimate facial expression, which seems to mean the same in every part of the world, is the smile. A true smile is never misunderstood and, as believed by some scientists, releases endorphins into the body that make us feel good. It also uses fewer muscles than a frown and therefore requires less energy!

Facial expression is so important that in order to avoid misunderstandings when sending e-mails, some of us accompany them with imitation faces.

Fig. 10.3
What are the faces in Figure 10.3 communicating?

Activity
Try to make the seven primary expressions of happiness, sadness, surprise, anger, fear, disgust and contempt.

Eye Contact

In western society, when we speak with someone face-to-face it is natural to look him in the eye. It is considered to show directness and integrity. Avoidance of eye contact shows lack of confidence and may indicate dishonesty. In the Czech Republic, avoiding eye contact when clinking beer glasses is interpreted as an indication that the person has something to hide and may not be trustworthy. In some Asian cultures however, eye contact can be considered rude.

Eye contact is also a way of communicating that we are listening. It lets the speaker know we are interested. It is also used as an initial means of contact. Prior to speaking to someone we usually make eye contact with him.

Eye contact communicates:

- Attitudes – intense gazing into another's eyes shows trust and closeness between two people. Is there a difference between gazing and staring into another's eyes?
- Attraction – our pupils involuntarily dilate when we are attracted to or interested in someone or something.
- Personality – assertive, confident and extrovert types make more direct eye contact than those who are less confident.
- Emotions – avoiding or breaking eye contact can show annoyance with someone.

Fig. 10.4 Eye contact.

Gesture

Gestures are actions we make with different parts of our body that can replace or support spoken communication. We each have hundreds of gestures that we use to communicate a vast array of messages.

Discussion

1. What messages can we send with each of the following parts of the body:
   - Head
   - Hands
   - Arms
   - Shoulders
   - Legs
   - Feet
2. How do we communicate the following using gestures:
   - Hello
   - Come here
   - Go away!
   - Stop
   - Money
   - OK
   - I don't know
   - Stupid!
   - Naughty!
   - Quiet
   - Drink?
   - Well done
   - Pleased to meet you

There are a multitude of gestures and gesture combinations. One gesture can have many different meanings, and there are many gestures that mean the same thing. Very subtle differences between similar gestures can have widely different meanings.

Discussion

What different meanings can the following have:
- A protruding tongue
- Hands up in the air
- The V-sign

By becoming more conscious of our gestures and by being clear in their transmission we can avoid vagueness and misunderstandings. It is useful to observe public speakers and the movements that they make when speaking. Be careful not to overdo gesturing to support speech as it may distract from what you are saying.

Activity

It is possible to have a 'conversation' using only gestures. Try to act out the following role-play without words:

A: Hello.
B: Hello.
A: Are you alright?
B: I'm alright. And you?
A: So so.
B: What time is it?
A: I don't know.
B: Can you give me some money?
A: No.
B: Please.
A: No!
B: I'm hungry.
A: I don't have any money!
B: I'm cold.
A: Look over there!
B: What, where? I don't see anything.
A: It doesn't matter.
B: Goodbye.
A: Bye.

Fig. 10.5 Brian Cowen using gestures during a speech.

 # Posture

How we stand, sit, walk, lie and generally hold our body communicates a variety of messages:

1. Mood and physical state, e.g. relaxed posture = confidence
2. How we feel towards others, e.g. two people squaring up to each other aggressively stand upright, shoulders back and head up straight.
3. Status, e.g. soldiers stand to attention in front of a superior officer; in some cultures they bow before royalty; people kneel to pray.
4. Situation, e.g. at an interview we sit upright showing alertness and interest.

Fig. 10.6 Rioters and police.
What messages are the different individuals in this picture sending out?

A look around a classroom often reveals a wide variety of moods from postures ranging from interest, to boredom to utter disbelief!

Territory

Our territory is something we feel strongly about and it can make us protective and defensive. It is our space and we communicate it in a variety of ways. Animals leave their scent on trees and bushes to let other animals know who lives there and humans mark their territory in visual ways.

There are three types of human territory: tribal, family and personal.

Tribal Territory

Primitive tribes occupied a specific area, consisting of a home base, and a hunting ground around it. Intruders would have been driven away and members of the tribe communicated their membership by war-chants and war-paint. Today, the tribe has become the nation, using non-verbal signals such as flags and national anthems to communicate its identity, and border checkpoints to show its boundary. Another example is football fans who communicate to rival fans their territory in the stadium with a display of colours, flags, scarves and chanting.

Family Territory

The family territory is the home, with the bedroom as the core where we feel most secure. People who have been burgled and had their private possessions in their bedrooms gone through, experience a sense of having been invaded. The house has a boundary of a wall, fence, or hedge. Within the home are other markers of territory: ornaments, furniture, family photographs, pictures on the walls etc. A family often displays its territory outside the home, when for example, there is a trip to the beach and towels, rugs, bags, etc. will mark the space to which it temporarily belongs.

Personal Territory

Each of us carries an invisible 'space bubble', our own portable piece of territory. We can see this when we get on to a bus or train. If the seats are all empty, except one, the chances are we won't sit next to the only person there. We will always sit where we give ourselves the maximum amount of space.

If someone unknown enters our bubble, we might feel threatened. If someone we know keeps well outside it we might feel rejected. Our personal space bubble communicates levels of formality, friendship, intimacy and how comfortable we feel with other people. We have to know someone pretty well, or trust her before we let her enter our space bubble. Sometimes we have no choice but to let others into our space, for example, at a crowded concert or football match. In Mediterranean and North African cultures they usually like to stand closer than Northern Europeans and Americans.

Sitting behind a desk is putting up a barrier, and therefore, distance, between two people. It can give the impression that we are unapproachable. Observe the different interview techniques of television chat show hosts. Some use desks and others don't. Which is more effective?

Activity

List five people you feel comfortable entering your 'space bubble'.
What do they have in common? Discuss your reasons with the class group.

Proximity

Proximity is how close we let someone get to us. It depends on:
1. Status – people of high status enter others' space more than vice versa, e.g. teacher and pupil, doctor and patient, Garda and criminal, officer and soldier, employer and employee.
2. Gender – women tend to be physically closer to each other than men.
3. Age – children enter each other's space more than adults.
4. Culture – Middle Eastern and African people get closer to each other than Westerners and some Asians.

 # Orientation

This is how we position ourselves in relation to others, and communicates how we feel towards them. We sit face-to-face with someone we like or respect. Giving someone the 'cold shoulder' means we face away from her in a display of dislike or disrespect.

Two people sitting at a table can choose to orient themselves in a number of different ways:

- Side by side
- Face-to-face across the table
- At right angles to each other at one corner

What are the differences between each of these in terms of formality and intimacy? Consider, for example, which is most appropriate for a job interview. Why did King Arthur have a round table? Consider the typical classroom set up. Are there alternative ways of arranging the seating for different types of activity?

Discussion

If a stranger approached you and appeared to be a threat, how would you orient yourself toward him/her? If he appeared to be no threat, how would your NVC be different?

Physical Contact

Experts say physical contact with others is good for us. It can satisfy emotional needs, increase our sense of self worth, and enhance our relationships as a means of communicating love, affection and closeness. Of course we all experience different degrees of closeness in our different relationships. For some people it would be perfectly natural to give an affectionate hug to a friend, while to others this would be an embarrassment. Touching defines relationships and communicates social status. What messages are being sent out by the people in these photographs? Is Bertie Ahern's physical contact with Romano Prodi appropriate?

Fig. 10.8 Physical Contact

Fig. 10.7 Physical Contact

There are four types of physical contact, ranging in degree of intimacy:
1. Functional – usually done in professional situations, e.g. doctors, physiotherapists, hairdressers.
2. Ritual – the most common type of ritual touching is the greeting, e.g. handshake, embrace, nose rub, kiss on the cheek, 'high five'.
3. Playful/supportive – used to indicate encouragement, sympathy and affection, e.g. pat on the back, touching the hand or arm. This type is open to misinterpretation, especially at work. It may be viewed as patronising, as an invasion of personal space or at worst as sexual harassment.
4. Intimate - between parent and child, between lovers.

Handshake Techniques

There are a variety of handshake techniques:
1. The firm handshake
2. The limp handshake
3. The accompanying hand on the other's elbow
4. The accompanying hand on the other's shoulder
5. The accompanying hand on the side of the other's head

Discussion

What does each of these handshake techniques communicate in terms of confidence, warmth and intimacy?

Physical contact varies in the following ways:
1. Status – doctors will touch patients and not vice versa (see proximity above).
2. Gender – women in western societies touch more than men.
3. Age – children touch more than older people.
4. Culture – Northern Europeans, Americans and Asians touch less than Southern Europeans and Africans. Many Asian societies are traditionally not touch oriented and public displays of affection are avoided.

Discussion

You have decided to go on a world trip for one year. At the airport a number or friends and family members have come to bid you farewell. How would you say goodbye to the following non-verbally:
• Your mother
• Your father
• Your sister
• Your brother
• Your closest friend
• A colleague
• Your boss

Paralanguage

Sometimes we communicate with the voice but not necessarily with words. There are three types:

1. Vocal qualities
2. Vocalisations
3. Vocal segregates

Vocal Qualities

- Pitch
- Volume
- Stress/emphasis
- Speed
- Rhythm
- Tone
- Accent

All of these can communicate our emotional state, personality, social class, origins, and level of education. We can alter the meaning of what we say by infusing it with different tones. We can convey approval or disapproval, warmth, humour, friendliness, dislike, scorn, sarcasm etc. We can sound serious or playful, firm, seductive, apologetic, angry etc.

If we are planning on working in a vocation that involves dealing with the public, it is important to be aware of how we speak. A warm welcoming tone to our voice is preferable than if we sound bored or impatient.

Activity

1. How would you say 'We have a half-day tomorrow,' as a question?
2. Try to say 'That's absolutely brilliant,' first using an enthusiastic, and then a sarcastic tone.
3. Try to say, 'Shush, be quiet' first in an angry, and then a gentle/friendly tone.

Vocalisations

Sometimes we communicate through noises rather than through speaking. We grunt, groan, moan, shriek, weep, gulp, giggle, laugh, snigger, cry, sigh, whisper, whistle, scream, shout, yawn, sneeze, cough, belch. As with other forms of NVC, they can be ambiguous, for example, what different meanings can a sigh communicate?

Vocal Segregates

The use of pause, hesitation and fillers like, 'Em'. Many of these we use unconsciously but using pause and hesitation effectively can greatly enhance a speech (see also Chapter 18).

- Admiration
- Derision
- Sexiness
- Cockiness
- Astonishment
Make up others if you wish.

Silence

In couples who are very close, silence communicates contentment as they may know each other so well they don't need to talk. On the other hand, it can mean awkwardness when two people cannot keep a conversation going. Giving someone the silent treatment is way of slighting someone we aren't pleased with. Teachers may use it to show disapproval in a classroom, usually accompanied by a stare. In many Asian countries silence indicates politeness and contemplation.

Depending on the situation silence can mean:
- Affection
- Reverence
- Attention
- Hesitation
- Embarrassment
- Hostility
- Oppression

The Environment

The design, shape, colour, size, temperature, lighting, smells and sound of place can affect how we feel and behave in a particular setting. In this way the environment communicates with us and we should be aware of how we arrange the furniture in a room for a meeting, for example. A room lit with daylight rather than artificial lighting can have a better effect on our work. A brightly lit room is easier to work in than a dark one, but dim lighting can create a romantic, or relaxing mood if that is what we want.

Restaurants use environmental factors to create atmospheres that can determine how long people stay. Fast food outlets use bright lights and not very comfortable seating to prompt customers to leave soon after they've finished eating. Soft music, candles, comfortable chairs are used in more expensive restaurants. Supermarkets have spent time and money researching how light and music affects how we shop.

Feng shui (pronounced fung shway) is an ancient Chinese way of arranging furniture, object and colours etc. so that we can feel more relaxed by a balanced energy.

Time

How we use time communicates something about relationships, status and personality. We tend to spend more time with people we like. An employer will spend more time with an employee who is impressive than with one who is less so. People of higher status tend to keep others waiting, e.g. a doctor will keep a patient waiting which tells us that the doctor's time is more precious. A person who is always late may be seen as being unreliable. In western society we are more concerned with punctuality than in many other cultures.

 # Music

It has been said that music can soothe the savage beast. In general it comes from and appeals to the emotions. It can soothe us, as the quote says, uplift us, invite us to dance, cause us to cry, fill us with joy, passion, anger etc. Listen to some different styles of music and try to identify what they are communicating in terms of mood and emotion. What do the following styles communicate to you:

• Rap
• Traditional Irish jig
• Psalm
• Punk
• Ambient
• Strauss waltz
• Heavy Metal
• Hip Hop
• Reggae
• Bach fugue
• Techno
• Folk ballad

Sounds

Bells, car horns, sirens, drum signals all communicate various messages.

Smell

Whether it comes from a person or a place, smells are powerful communicators, usually either attracting or repelling. The aroma of fine food wafting from a restaurant, the sweet perfume of flowers on a May day, smoke from our clothes after we've been in a bar the previous night all provoke emotional responses and give out their own messages. Even though we have lost much of the power of our sense of smell, we still tend to cover up our own unpleasant odours with different soaps, perfumes and oils to make ourselves socially accepted, or to try and attract a partner. We might even de-odorise our homes to make them more pleasant to inhabit.

Dance

Dance is an artistic expression using many of the non-verbal techniques mentioned above such as posture and gesture, but it is also much more than that. A famous ballet like 'Swan Lake' is a powerful performance full of emotion and drama. 'Riverdance' recently changed traditional Irish dancing into something much more passionate than it used to be and introduced it to a worldwide audience. What does it communicate to you?

Art

Painting, drawing and sculpture are all forms of visual art. They can communicate any number of moods, feelings and ideas, or may just be something attractive to hang on the wall.

Other NVC Signs and Codes

Morse code, semaphore, drum signals, smoke signals, traffic lights and some road signs all use non-verbal ways of communicating messages. Computer technology uses languages that are based on number as opposed to words and programs are written in a series of 0s and 1s. Shorthand is a system of written symbols used to record speech quickly.

Activities

1. Role-play the following simple situations using only NVC:
   - Waiting at the bus stop in freezing weather.
   - A tourist asking directions (doesn't speak the language).
   - A mugging.
   - Football supporters at a match in the minutes leading up to and including a goal.
   - Ordering a meal in a restaurant.
2. Try to spend a break session without using words.
3. Chinese Miming

   You may have played Chinese whispers before. This is similar. Everyone sits in a circle, and the first person sends a message by mime to the person on her left. That person passes it on to the person on his left and so on around the circle. Compare the final message to the original.
4. Four secretaries working at their computers. A large window is between them and the street. A man tries to pick each one up by knocking on the window to try and get them to come outside. Each secretary reacts differently.

 # Chapter Review

1. Give a brief explanation of: eye contact; face-to-face communication and facial expression; gestures; territory; paralanguage.
2. Explain the significance of NVC with regard to cultural differences.
3. Describe ways in which NVC can be ambiguous.
4. Make a list of the NVC types you are now more aware of and consider how you might consciously use them in future.

Chapter 11 Visual Communiation

The Image

Verbal communication uses words to send messages; visual communication uses images. The image is a very powerful means of communication. Some people have called the twentieth century the century of the image. For centuries the written word was a primary means of finding out about the world but with the emergence of photography, cinema, television, video and the Internet the image has almost overtaken the written word as a means of communication.

Today we are constantly being bombarded by visual messages.

Discussion

What are the various merits and demerits of visual and written communication in terms of reliability, accuracy, interest?

We can often read and understand a visual message more quickly than a written one. An image is easier to remember than words and can cross linguistics barriers. It may also have much more immediate and emotional impact.

Fig. 11.1 Running from napalm attack.
This photograph by Nick Ut of Phan Thi Kim Phuc had a profound effect on American public opinion of the Vietnam War.

Discussion

There is an old saying that 'a picture is worth a thousand words'. What does this mean? Could we ever say that a word is worth a thousand pictures?

Images should not be seen as being superior to words but as equally important. The most successful communication is when there is a combination of words and pictures. Some images on their own can be ambiguous and even meaningless. This is why captions are used to explain photographs in newspapers and magazines, and slogans accompany pictures used in advertisements. In this way, words *anchor* the meaning of the image. Words and images complement each other and should be carefully chosen. Look at a cover of *Phoenix* or *Private Eye* magazine to see how humour is created out of inserting slightly inappropriate, but often hilarious, speech bubbles into photographs of celebrities and politicians.

Fig. 11.2 Phoenix magazine cover.

Visual communication also has the power to manipulate, especially in the modern media. Photography, film, television and video as media communication are deliberately manipulated to produce a specific effect on the viewer. It may be to persuade him to buy a product, to make him laugh or cry, to seduce him into wanting to watch another episode or just wonder at the beauty of the image. It used to be said that the camera never lies, but it does, very effectively.

One major disadvantage to visual communication is that images cannot give detailed descriptions, which words can. Nor can they express abstract ideas like hope, fate or knowledge or complex feelings like resentment or rejection. It is easier to visualise words that refer to concrete objects, such as dog, ball and hat.

Visual Language

Verbal language has rules of grammar and punctuation in order to give it meaning. We don't usually consider visual language to have such rules but we can look at some of the basic elements of visual communication. These are:

- Colour/light
- Form/shape
- Size
- Texture
- Depth
- Perspective
- Boundaries
- Position
- Movement/direction

Colour

Colour is essentially a combination of different shades of light and dark and it can communicate a variety of meanings. Light and darkness can affect our moods, lightness being linked with daytime, spring and summer, positive feelings of hope, celebration and joy. Darkness we associate with night-time, winter and negative feelings of fear, despair and depression. Not everyone will have the same feelings of course. Some people love dark colours and wear them all the time. They can look smart and sophisticated. How we view colour is highly subjective.

Discussion

1. In the film *Reservoir Dogs* the chief characters were named after colours, Mr White, Mr Black etc. The two unpopular colours were Mr Pink and Mr Brown. Why did no one want to be called by these names? Why was there competition for the name Mr Black?
2. What words, feelings and ideas do you associate with these colours:
   - Red
   - Orange
   - Yellow
   - Green
   - Blue
   - White

When using colour in a visual message we must remember that it can affect the emotions of a viewer more than other attributes. If used well it can draw attention to certain aspects of an image. If poorly used it can damage the overall effect.

Size

In image production, size counts. We tend to notice large images more easily than smaller ones. When designing an image we need to consider its size in relation to the page on which it will appear.

Texture

Texture refers to the feel or appearance of a surface, or of an image. Look at the table or desk nearest to you. Is its surface rough or smooth, is its colour plain or dappled?

Depth

We perceive the world as having three dimensions. In other words we can see the actual volume of objects which show that they have weight and mass. A square, a circle and a triangle each have two dimensions, but a cube, a sphere and a pyramid each have three.

Perspective

Perspective gives the impression of distance in a picture. A picture of a railway track disappearing into the distance shows perspective by the way the lines get closer together as they 'get further away'.

Boundaries

The boundary of an image is the edge or frame that contains it. Borderlines or designs can enhance a poster but they can also distract from the main image if they are too prominent.

Position

The positioning of an image in relation to the boundary is quite important. The most obvious thing is to place an image in the centre. When taking photographs of people, we often 'cut off' their feet, or the tops of their heads by mistake. Filling the frame of a photograph means not having the object too far away or chopped in two. Do we want just someone's face, or their entire body in the picture?

Movement/direction

Getting a viewer to perceive movement in a still image needs 'visual vibration'. The use of wavy lines is applied to cartoons to show a character moving or shaking, and high-contrast straight or wavy lines can create the illusion of something moving in a particular direction.

Fig. 11.3 Movement.

Visual Interpretation

As with all forms of communication, an image can have more than one specified meaning. The meaning is determined by a combination of the sender, receiver and the context. A national flag is literally a symbol of the country it represents. It can also fill one person with patriotic pride, but to another, it could represent an offence or a threat. A Union Jack in the Falls Road in Belfast will have a completely different meaning to one hanging in the Shankill Road. As well as the literal meaning, there is an implied meaning, or connotation.

Activity
What is the connotation of the photograph below?

Fig. 11.4 President Bush in 'Climate Accident'.

Symbols

A symbol is a particular kind of image or sign that represents or is associated with something. Because the meaning is not always obvious, we usually have to learn it. Logos, flags, religious images and numbers are all examples of symbols.

Visual Production

Many of us are daunted by the prospect of having to produce a visual message. We think we can't paint or draw, and wonder where we will get any inspiration. Firstly, remember that you don't have to be an artist or a designer to produce an effective image. Visual quotation is perhaps a slightly elaborate way to describe 'borrowing' existing signs or images and adding something or reshaping them to make them our own. Many advertisements use this technique because advertisers understand that we notice what is already familiar to us.

Images on the Internet

The Internet is a rich fishing ground for images of almost anything we care to imagine. To copy an image from a web page, simply move the mouse so that the cursor is on the image. Right click the mouse. A box with various instructions will appear. Left click on Copy. Now open up a new document, and under Edit, click Paste and the image will reappear in your document. This can be altered in shape and size to suit your needs. Remember that cropping (cutting off part of a picture) can radically change its meaning.

Other Media

Books, newspapers and magazines are also full of photographs, pictures and diagrams that we can borrow although take care you don't break any rules of copyright. An effective type of image is a collage of pictures, materials, words or even items of rubbish arranged and fixed to a backing. They may relate to a specific theme, or they could form an original shape or image of their own.

Posters and Flyers

These can be easily done either by hand or on a computer, using readily available programs. A poster must be large, preferably A2 size, and should have sufficient impact that will compete with a range of other visual stimuli in a busy urban environment. It has to communicate immediately with a passer-by, who usually has little time to stop and look at the details, therefore the image has to be simple and striking. Too much detail will put people off, and the communication will fail. Some designers deliberately create provocative images to enhance their effect. Many Benetton advertisements are notoriously controversial, but they succeed in grabbing our attention.

A flyer, normally printed on A5 sized paper, is often placed directly into our hand or through our letterbox and we have time to read the details. More text can be used on a flyer than a poster. Often posters are simply enlarged flyers.

Greeting Cards

There are a number of types of greeting card that we send and receive throughout the year. Since they are sent directly to people they are not competing for attention. Again, a computer can assist in the production of a card. However, a card, by virtue of its name, means it is on a piece of card and not just paper. There are obvious images associated with different occasions, festivals and holidays.

Font Selection

Look at the following list of film titles. Is there anything strange about them? We have seen the titles written before but the way they are written seems to be at odds with the themes of the films. *Frankenstein* is a horror film, yet the font used is humorous and playful. The connotations of the film are monsters, mad scientists, Middle Europe in the eighteenth century and the font does not suit these connotations. Make a similar analysis of the other titles, their connotations and the fonts used.

FRANKENSTEIN   The Wizard of Oz   **Shakespeare in Love**   *Pulp Fiction*

If you are using text to accompany an image, choose a font that is appropriate for the message.

Data Representation

Charts, graphs and diagrams are very useful for showing statistics in a simple and interesting way. They can give written assignments, projects and oral presentations a bit of added impact and interest, condensing and clarifying certain types of information. A computer makes them fairly easy to produce with a range of styles and colours and even three-dimensional effects.

Line graphs are useful for showing trends that rise and fall.

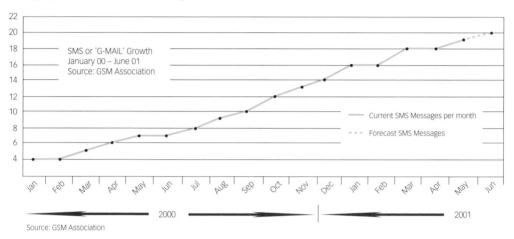

Source: GSM Association

Fig. 11.6 Line graph.

Bar charts are effective for illustrating differences in quantity. They can be horizontal or vertical.

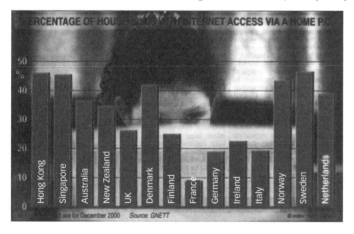

Fig. 11.7 Bar chart.

Histograms are similar to bar charts, except the columns represent the frequency of occurrence (how often something occurs) and have no spaces between them.

Pie charts can be used to display percentages of a whole.

Breakdown of worldwide Internet users by region, September 1999

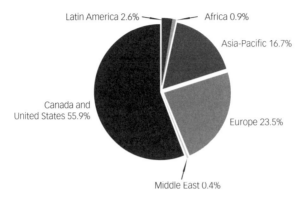

Source: Nua Internet Surveys

Total Number of users: 201 million

Fig. 11.8 Pie chart.

Pictograms, as the name suggests, consists of a picture or series of pictures that can add a touch of humour, although they are not as precise as other kinds of chart.

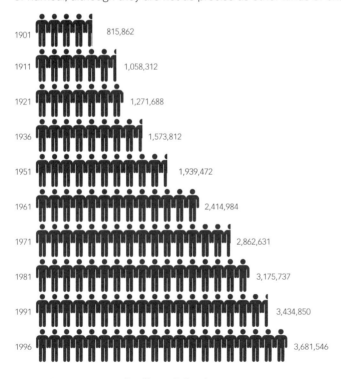

1901 How New Zealand's Poulation has grown

Source: Statistics New Zealand, Facts and Figures 1998

Fig. 11.9 Pictogram.

The following three are not strictly visual, but they do help simplify information:

Organisation charts are used to show the structure of authority in an organisation.

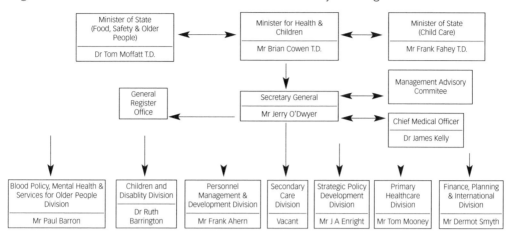

Source: Department of Health and Children

Fig. 11.10 Organisation chart.

Flow charts show how an activity is to be carried out in a series of logical stages.

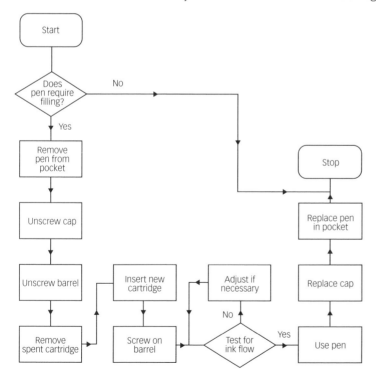

Source: Purves, Brian, Information Graphics, 1987

Fig. 11.11 Flow chart.

Tables can be used to compare and contrast data in a clear and simple way.

Average Weekday – Listened Yesterday – Adults National

	Jan / June 2000	Apr / Sept 2000	Diff
	%	%	% points
Any Radio	89	89	n/c
Any RTE1 / 2 FM / Lyric	54	54	n/c
Radio 1	30	30	n/c
2 FM	28	29	+1
Lyric fm	3	3	n/c
Any Local	54	55	+1
Home Local	50	50	n/c
Today FM	14	15	+1

Source: JNLR/MRBI 1990/00 & April – Sept 00 (Interim Report)

Fig. 11.12 Table.

Points to Remember

1. Always title charts
2. Keep them simple and clear
3. Don't clutter them with too much information
4. Colour looks better than black and white
5. Keep text to a minimum and make it legible
6. Fill up as much of the page as possible

Diagrams

A diagram is essentially a drawing or sketch of an object showing its various parts. It would obviously be preferable to see a diagram of the inner workings of a camera than have someone try to explain them to us!

Maps

To show locations, transport networks, or any geographical features, maps are ideal.

Eight Steps to Creating a Visual Message

1. Decide on a communication objective. What do you want to communicate? Do you want to send a message of great meaning and importance, or to entertain, educate, inform, advertise or would you prefer to express yourself artistically, if so inclined?

2. Decide on an appropriate visual medium/format. What materials will you use and why? These two may be done in reverse if you already know what medium you want to use but are not yet sure of the message.
3. Decide who is your target audience.
4. Develop your idea. Do a rough sketch/outline. Decide on colours, shapes, size, texture etc.
5. Refine and polish.
6. Decide if it needs text/verbal support. Keep it short and simple. Choose an appropriate font.
7. Test its impact on your friends/classmates/tutors.

Presenting a Visual Assignment

When presenting a visual assignment it will be important to submit support studies to show a record of the process. It should include the following:
1. Written notes recording the process, i.e. the development of your ideas from start to finish - where you got the idea and why you chose it
2. Your communication objective
3. Reasons for choosing your medium/materials
4. Rough sketches/outlines
5. Description of any changes and alterations made during the rough work
6. Reasons you made them
7. What you liked/disliked about your initial ideas sketches
8. On submission of the final piece, you should include all rough work and the written record.

Assessment Activities

1. Produce a poster and/or flyer for one of the following:
   - A concert
   - A newly opened leisure centre/restaurant/shop/business
   - A college social
   - A sporting event
   - A fashion show
   - A circus
   - A charity/fundraising event
   - An international day against racism
   - An international day of AIDS awareness

   Think of other occasions, perhaps related to your own vocational studies.

2. Produce a card for one of the following occasions:
   - Birthday
   - Christmas
   - Passing exams
   - Wedding Anniversary
   - Condolence

- St Patrick's Day
- St Valentine's Day
- Easter
- New born baby
- Mother's Day
- Father's Day

 Chapter Review

1. What advantages does visual communication have over verbal communication?
2. Why is it important to learn about visual communication?

Part 4

Interpersonal
Communication

Chapter 12 Interpersonal Communication

FETAC Assessment Requirements
Preparation for Dialogue, Discussion, Group Work, Meetings and Oral Presentation

Topics Covered

Empathy

Dual Perspective

Communication Climate

Self-Disclosure

Acceptance/Non-Acceptance

Conflict

Aggressive/Passive/Assertive Behaviour

In this chapter we will look at the foundations of interpersonal communication, exploring the way communication can help create healthy relationships, whether they are to do with business or work; friendships or close intimate relationships.

 # Empathy

As a sender of a message we need to take into account the receiver – her values, beliefs, emotional state, level of understanding etc. Empathy means being able to feel what another person is feeling. This is not always possible but we can come close by *trying* to understand where she is coming from.

Dual Perspective

Dual perspective means that while we recognise and take into account another person's point of view when we communicate with her, we also have to be aware of our own perspective.

Communication Climate

According to Julia Wood in her book, *Communication in our Lives*, communication climate is the general feeling or mood between people in interpersonal communication. Sometimes we may feel intense, nervous or defensive with someone and this will have a negative impact on the way we talk to him. At other times we may feel relaxed and friendly and we will be inclined to talk more openly. This can have an effect on communication in many different contexts, for example, at work the atmosphere should be supportive and productive so that it encourages good working relationships and results. In social situations it is important that we can feel relaxed and that we can unwind with our friends. In close personal relationships the climate should be suitable for us to be able to express our opinions and feelings without being criticised or ridiculed.

Self-Disclosure

'Self-disclosure is revealing personal information about ourselves that others are unlikely to discover on their own.' (Wood, 2000, p.194). Revealing our innermost selves is not something we do everyday with everybody. However in certain circumstances it can create closeness between people. By sharing our personal thoughts, feelings and experiences with another he may come to understand us better. It can also invite others to self-disclose to us. Often there are things that we have experienced or done, which make us embarrassed or ashamed. By disclosing these to another person, and having them accepted without criticism, we can come to accept ourselves more easily. Obviously there has to be a certain level of trust already between two people before they engage in self-disclosure, but we should not be afraid to enter unfamiliar territory by trying out new and different ways of communicating. This can lead us to learn more about ourselves and ultimately to personal growth.

There are different levels of self-disclosure, depending on how long we have known a person. Initially we tend to reveal superficial information about ourselves: where we're from, our tastes and what we do in our spare time. If response to initial disclosures is positive (the other person withholds criticism and doesn't reveal them to others) and reciprocal (he reveals the same sort of information), we feel secure and will tend to reveal more intimate details. We might tell him about our family background, what we're good and not so good at and our own relationship experiences. As a relationship develops, there is less and less need to self-disclose as we get to know the other person better and a bond of trust is formed.

Discussion

1. What are the benefits and risks of self-disclosure?
2. A friend of mine recently moved to Ennis in County Clare. He went to a pub for a drink and took a seat. He said to a man sitting nearby, 'How's it going?' to which the man replied, 'I had a heart by-pass operation in 1989.' Is this appropriate self-disclosure?

Activity

We need to know what sort of self-disclosure is appropriate in different contexts. In groups of three or four, discuss and then write down in which of the following contexts you would reveal each type of information:

Contexts	Information
Job Interview	Personal habits
Meeting someone in a doctor's waiting room	Recreational pursuits
Meeting someone at a party	Information about sexual relationships
On a first date	Information about experiences with drugs
With work colleagues	Career ambitions
With an authority figure, e.g. employer	Medical history
At dinner with friends	Dreams
At dinner with the family	Feelings about thorny issues like abortion
With a close friend	Feelings about your family
With a casual acquaintance	Religious beliefs
	Political preferences
	Fantasies
	Favourite foods
	Personal achievements
	Personal weaknesses/faults
	Confessions

Discussion

Consider what affects your decision to disclose or not? Is it the information or the context/people involved? Would you disclose similar information in a chat room or online? What kinds of situations prevent certain types of information being revealed? Are there topics that are taboo in certain situations?

Everyone will have slightly different standards for self-disclosure. If it is practised effectively it can help create an open and comfortable communication climate.

Acceptance and Non-acceptance

No one likes to feel unaccepted. Many of us have experienced standing at a busy shop counter or at a bar, waiting to be served and feeling that we are being ignored. Messages can be either accepting or non-accepting, in other words they can communicate whether or not we recognise, acknowledge or approve of the person with whom we are interacting. This can have a powerful effect on the communication climate. Being ignored is receiving a non-accepting message.

Acceptance

Studies have devised three basic forms of acceptance:

1. Recognition
2. Acknowledgment
3. Approval

Acceptance is communicated by:

1. Recognition of someone's existence using eye contact, a handshake, a smile or a simple greeting.
2. Acknowledgment of their thoughts and feelings by showing we are listening by head nods, eye contact, 'Uh huh' and 'Yes' responses.
3. Approval of their thoughts and feelings by saying something like, 'I know what you mean'.

Non-acceptance

Non-acceptance is communicated by:

1. Non-recognition of someone's existence by avoiding eye contact, ignoring someone or remaining silent.
2. Not acknowledging someone's thoughts and feelings by ignoring their expression of these, e.g.
   'I'm having difficulties with Bill,'
   'Oh really? Where's my pencil?'
3. Disapproval of someone's thoughts and feelings by contradiction, e.g.
   'I'm having difficulties with Bill,'
   'Don't be stupid. You're imagining things.'

Discussion

Discuss your own experiences in which you were accepted or non-accepted. What effects did they have on your relationships?

Activity

In groups of two to four, develop the following simple role-plays. For each suggested role-play give an example of both *acceptance* and *non-acceptance*.

Alternatively, make up your own scenarios.

1. Recognition
    - Three people are in a room and someone else enters.
    - A customer tries to get the attention of a sales assistant/barman.
    - A tourist trying to stop someone in the street to ask directions.
2. Acknowledgment
    - At a group meeting one person is trying to put forward plans about a social night.
    - At a party a group of friends are having a chat. One says he/she is being pestered by someone.
    - Two colleagues are having a talk about work. One says he/she thinks the lunch breaks of forty minutes are too short.
3. Approval
    - Discussion between two friends one of whom has just joined a religious group/started seeing someone new.
    - Two colleagues at work discussing another colleague who is always late.

Discuss the role-plays afterwards. How does it feel to be at the receiving end of a message that does not accept you?

Other Influences on Communication Climate

An *unhealthy* communication climate results from statements that:

1. Are judgmental
2. Disrespect others
3. Are controlling
4. Don't allow other points of view

A *healthy* communication climate results from statements that:

1. Are non-judgmental
2. Treat others with respect
3. Are collaborative
4. Allow other points of view

Activity

1. In the following pairs of statements, which would promote a healthy and which would promote an unhealthy communication climate:

   You don't work as hard as you could.
   You're so lazy.

   Maybe we should discuss this.
   It's pointless to discuss this any further.

   That idea was tried before and it didn't succeed.
   That's a stupid idea.

   Your assignment was crap.
   Your writing skills need improving and there is insufficient research in your assignment.

   Refugees are just scroungers, end of story.
   Many refugees have to resort to begging to survive.

   We're not having the social on that date, end of discussion.
   I'm not so sure about that date, what does anyone else think?

   You'll do it my way because I pay you.
   What about doing it this way?

2. Which of the following statements could promote an unhealthy communication climate:
   (a) I don't want to talk about it.
   (b) Who asked you?
   (c) That's not what I said.
   (d) I used to think like that.
   (e) So what?
   (f) I think you should take a break.
   (g) Don't be an idiot.
   (h) I'd like to discuss this later.
   (i) I disagree.
   (j) You're talking rubbish.
   (k) You'll never amount to anything.
   (l) I can't imagine how you must feel.
   (m) I appreciate what you're saying, but we should explore other possibilities.
   (n) You're a liar.
   (o) Can I talk to you?
   (p) I heard something very different.

(q) I don't care what you think.
(r) We aren't getting anywhere.
(s) You could have a point there.

3. The following statements could promote an unhealthy communication climate. Change them into statements that would promote a more supportive healthy one:
(a) You're a terrible player.
(b) That repair job you did on my wall is just rubbish.
(c) You eejit. You spilled my drink.
(d) You couldn't drive to save your life.
(e) Can I talk to someone else, you're useless.
(f) Can't you look where you're going? You stupid fool.
(g) Why are you going to college? It's a waste of time.
(h) You're always late.
(i) Politicians are all liars.
(j) You're going to fail your exams.
(k) If we don't do it my way, then forget about it.

Conflict

Conflict results from having different interests, priorities, goals and views from others. It is inevitable in personal and professional relationships, yet it doesn't have to result in a break in those relationships. Often it can be a healthy indication that people are really involved with each other and that there is a strong connection between them.

Overt Conflict

Overt conflict is when we express our disagreements openly and honestly. We may do it quietly and calmly or we may have an enormous row. Either way, the differences are aired in the open.

Covert Conflict

Covert conflict is when we express our differences indirectly. For example, if we are annoyed with our partner because she turned up late for an assignation, and we decide we will do the same to her the next time. This is not dealing with the problem openly and problems are likely to remain unresolved. It is healthier to solve differences when they are communicated openly.

Responding to Conflict

Depending on how we respond to conflict, it can strengthen a relationship or break it apart. Responses to conflict can be:

1. Active – we do something about it

2. Passive – we do nothing about it
3. Constructive – we aim to preserve and maintain the relationship
4. Destructive – we aim to break up the relationship

There are four *specific* responses to conflict which use combinations of the above responses:

1. *Exit* is when we leave either literally, or psychologically by saying, 'I don't want to talk about it.' It is *active*, because action is taken and *destructive* because it damages the relationship.
2. *Neglect* is when we deny there is a problem. We might say, 'You're imagining things.' This response is *passive* since nothing is done to help the situation and it is also *destructive*.
3. *Loyalty* is when we believe that the situation will improve on its own. It often occurs in relationships in which one partner has a problem, and out of loyalty the other decides to stay. It is *passive* because no action is taken and *constructive* because there is the desire to preserve the relationship.
4. *Voice*, as the name implies, involves trying to discuss the problem openly, and at the same time preserving the relationship. It is both *active* and *constructive* and is the ideal way of dealing with conflict.

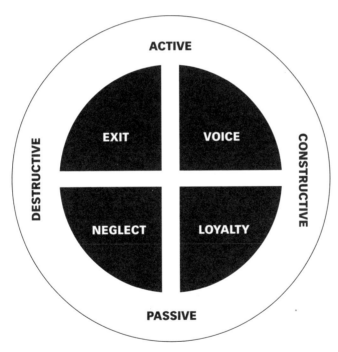

Fig. 12.1 Model of responses to conflict.
(Wood, p.209)

It is useful to recognise our own tendencies for dealing with conflict, and to decide whether they are healthy or not. If not, we should consider developing alternative ways of dealing with it. We also need to recognise that conflict need not always be destructive. It can be a useful tool for personal growth as we become aware of our own needs and ideas. It can also help us to see and consider other people's points of view that may be different from our own. Too much conflict in our lives can be unhealthy and stressful. If we treat others with mistrust, only see our own viewpoint, keep on the defensive and always use the same style of communication to deal with situations, then we will experience more conflict than is healthy. By adopting some of these communication techniques, we can reduce conflict in our lives.

Activity

In groups of two or three, discuss how each of you has dealt with one experience involving conflict. Was it successful? Have one person in each group take notes. From the notes, discuss with the whole class group. Select one or two for role-play and adapt them so that they deal with the conflict in an appropriate way.

I-/You-Statements

Conflict often arises because we blame others for the way we feel. Unless we are in an unhealthy or dysfunctional relationship in which someone is actually harming us, a lot of the time we blame other people for what are really our own responses to what they have said. Other people are seldom the cause of our feelings. Language that puts the blame on others often begins with 'You':

• 'You're doing my head in.'
• 'You're so demanding.'
• 'You get on my nerves.'
• 'You're being horrible to me.'

Blaming others for the way we feel is likely to make them defensive and conflict can result. However, if we take responsibility for the way we feel by using 'I' language we will help diffuse conflict situations.

I-statements	You-statements
Take responsibility for our own feelings	Put the responsibility onto another person
Put us in control of our feelings	Imply someone else controls our feelings
Are descriptive	Are vague and sometimes judgemental
Don't blame another person	Blame someone else
Can defuse conflict	Can create conflict
Are more open	Are less open

Activity

Compare the following pairs of statements:

You're intimidating me.
I feel intimidated by you.

You're doing my head in.
I get really annoyed when you do that.

You humiliated me.
I felt humiliated when you did that.

You hurt my feelings.
I felt hurt when you said that.

You're so demanding.
I can't cope with these demands.

You get on my nerves.
I feel irritated by you.

I-statements may feel strange when we use them for the first time. It can feel like we are being submissive whereas in fact it is empowering, putting us in control of ourselves as opposed to others. It is communication that is open and honest and leaves room for further discussion.

Observe your own use of 'You-statements' in relationships and slowly try to incorporate 'I-statements' instead. Discuss your experiences with the class.

Activity

Role-play: Four flatmates: A, B, C and D are discussing their living together.

A is a student; found the flat in the first place, but is always late with the rent, which annoys the landlady who threatens to evict them.

B works in a supermarket; owns the television set, but never does any washing up.

C is unemployed; watches a lot of television and frequently has friends around that the others don't like, but does most of the cleaning.

D is a nurse, who does shift work. She smokes and drinks a lot and makes a racket till all hours and owns the stereo and most of the CDs.

The discussion begins with news that the landlady has threatened to evict you if you are late with the rent again. You must reach agreement at the end that you will all try harder and remain living together. Observe the use of I- and you-statements and evaluate with the full class group when/where in the role-play these statements were used and how it felt both to use them and to hear them.

Aggressive/Passive/Assertive Behaviour

Aggressive Behaviour
- Forces one's needs, ideas and feelings upon another person
- Results in a win-lose situation, the aggressor winning by force
- Puts one's own ideas and rights before others'
- Does not listen to others' points of view
- Is arrogance

Passive Behaviour
- Is sacrificing our own needs, ideas and feelings for the sake of another
- Is frequently apologetic and lacks initiative
- Doesn't stand up for rights
- Puts other's rights before one's own
- Results in a lose-win situation, the passive person losing

Assertive Behaviour
- Is a positive and useful way of expressing our own ideas, needs and feelings without putting them above those of others
- Is a way of dealing with conflict successfully
- Should result in win-win situations, in other words no one loses
- Is a belief in one's own ideas and views but also recognises others' rights
- Attempts to arrive at a situation acceptable to both sides

Discussion
A colleague at work is constantly asking you to make him cups of coffee. One day he does it when you are extremely busy.
Aggressive response: 'Get it yourself you lazy slob. Can't you see I'm busy?'
Passive response: 'Well...actually, I'm aah...oh alright I'll get it for you.'
Assertive response: 'I'm a little busy at the moment. Couldn't you get it yourself?'
  Discuss these responses. What effect will each have on the speaker, the listener, and the pattern of behaviour?

Activity
In groups of three or four discuss situations in which you find it difficult to assert yourself. Have one person take notes in the group. From the notes taken, discuss the situations with the whole group. Choose one or two of the situations for role-play and adapt them so that appropriate assertive behaviour is displayed.

Chapter Review

1. Give a brief explanation of empathy and dual perspective.
2. Explain what is meant by communication climate.
3. What are the advantages and disadvantages of self-disclosure?
4. Give three examples each of accepting and non-accepting communication.
5. What are the advantages and disadvantages of conflict?
6. Outline the four responses to conflict.
7. Explain the significance of I-language.
8. Give a brief explanation of aggressive, passive and assertive behaviour.

Part 5

The Spoken Word

Chapter 13 Listening

We Can't Close Our Ears

Listening is the first communication skill we practise as infants, and from listening to other people around us, we learn how to speak. We listen far more than we speak, read or write; possibly up to 75% of the time, yet it is a communication skill we are not formally taught. We can close our eyes and mouths and can leave the keyboard or pen alone, but our ears are constantly open. We are frequently told to 'listen up,' that we 'weren't listening,' that we 'never listen,' but we are seldom taught *how* to listen effectively.

Listening consists of three components:

1. Hearing – the ability to perceive sounds
2. Understanding – the ability to make sense of those sounds
3. Retaining – the ability to remember what has been heard

Listening and Hearing

Listening is a skill of perception that helps us make sense of the world. Like perception, we select what we want to listen to. From where you are sitting now, concentrate for a few moments on all of the sounds you can hear and make a note of them. How many of them were you actually aware of without concentrating on them? Probably very few. How many of them could you make sense of? All of them? This illustrates the difference between listening and hearing. We can *hear* many things going on around us but it is only when we *make sense* of them and *understand* them that we are *listening* to them. It isn't practical to listen to everything we can hear. It would also be exhausting. Listening is an active skill, which requires a certain amount of concentration, whereas hearing is passive. Effective listening isn't always easy, but it is a skill that can be learnt.

Types of Listening

Julia Wood (2000, p. 184) lists five types of listening:

Informational Listening

This involves listening for information, for facts, times, names, places etc. It is the most common type of listening that we do most of the time.

Critical Listening

Critical listening entails making judgments, evaluations and forming opinions of a speaker's ideas. A teacher evaluates a student's oral presentation by listening critically for signs of careful preparation, structure, accurate information and good expression.

Relational Listening

Relational listening refers to the empathising we do when, for example, we are listening to a friend discuss his problems or worries. Relational listening often involves trying to understand another's feelings and interpreting signs that are hidden behind the information we hear.

Listening for Pleasure

Listening for pleasure is what we do when we play a CD, go to a concert, poetry reading or a comedy show. This normally doesn't need too much concentration unless we want to focus on specifics like a lyric or a drum beat in a song.

Listening to Discriminate

This is what a mechanic does when fine tuning an engine, detecting the subtle difference in sounds, or when parents decide if a child's crying is due to hunger, discomfort, a need for attention or a nappy change.

 # Barriers to Listening

To try to improve our listening techniques, we must first isolate the problems that prevent us from listening. Here are some of the most common ones:

- Poor physical or mental state, e.g. if we are hungry, cold, tired or anxious
- Disinterest in the speaker or subject
- Prejudice or hasty judgments about the speaker's appearance, accent, command of the language
- Prejudice about the subject, e.g. 'I disagree with her views so why should I bother paying attention?'
- Noise and distractions from the surrounding environment
- Daydreaming and thinking of things from the recent past or immediate future, e.g. 'what she said to me at break' or 'what I'm going to have for lunch'
- Inability to understand what the speaker is saying
- The speaker's speed, e.g. too slow – we may get bored; too fast – we may not be able to follow what is being said
- The message is too complex or unclear
- Attention span, e.g. if we develop an 'MTV' attention span of approximately 3-4 minutes, how can we concentrate and listen effectively for an entire hour? The average person can concentrate comfortably for approximately twenty minutes. There are also particular times of the day at which we may find it harder or easier to concentrate – some people are morning people, others are more alert at night time
- Impatience

Activity

Look at the list below. Imagine you have to listen to each of the people on the list and try to honestly assess your listening ability using a scale of 0 (very poor) to 10 (excellent) in each case:

- Your boss giving you instructions
- Someone you're trying to impress telling you about herself
- A teacher you like (in class)
- A teacher you don't like (in class)
- Your parents reprimanding you
- A child telling you about his day at school

Selective Listening

We tend to pick and choose to whom and to what we want to listen. For the most part, we give our attention to people and subjects that we are interested in. Or we focus on individuals and things that can benefit us, and the rest we frequently ignore. However when we're listening to important messages that need to be passed on to someone else, we have to select the important information and omit the rest.

Activity

Have someone read the following and note down the relevant points:
Ms Dunne, Sheila, not Sandra, had an appointment for 16.30 on Wednesday 26 June. She has since discovered that it clashes with a dental appointment in Clonskeagh, with Mr Flynn who graduated from university in 1987, coming 4th out of a class of 26. She would like to change her appointment to Thursday 4 July at 9.45, when she was expecting to bring her dog, Boris, to the vet, but he died on Monday 17 June of mange, and she buried him the following Tuesday. Please call her back at 087 5992600, between 15.00 and 22.00 on weekdays or anytime at weekends except between 10 and 12 noon on Sundays when she goes to Mass with her daughter Doris.

Active Listening

We should show the speaker that we're listening by giving verbal or non-verbal feedback. We can say 'Yes' or 'OK' or simply nod. This has the effect of encouraging the speaker to communicate. It's like telling a joke and everyone laughs. We feel encouraged to tell another. If no one laughs we usually stop. By giving feedback we are keeping focussed on the message, which helps us to listen and we are also giving encouragement to the speaker. This makes the communication more effective.

Interrupting

Interrupting a speaker is often considered bad manners and can cause conflict. It can indicate that we have not been listening, are not interested or believe what we have to say is more important. However there are occasions when interrupting is just about the cut and thrust of conversation. During political debates on television or radio, we hear members of a panel say, 'If I can be allowed to finish…' We should always let someone finish her point before making our own contribution.

 # Responsive Listening

Sometimes our ability to listen is diminished by our emotional state. For example, someone may be upset or annoyed by something, and may not want to listen to us even if we try to calm him down, or explain the problem to him. When we try to do this, he often gets more upset because he feels he is not being listened to. What we should do is accept his feelings, respond to them and then give our message. This lets him know we have listened to and understood the message.

Activity

Imagine how each of these dialogues might continue:

Example 1

Mother to child:
'No you can't stay up and play computer games anymore. It's time for bed and that's that.'

Mother to child:
'I know that you want to stay up late and play computer games because it's great fun, but you've already been on the computer for two hours and I'm worried that you'll be tired tomorrow for school. That's why I think you should go to bed now.'

Example 2

Boss to employee:
'No you can't have the day off tomorrow. Our new clients are coming for a meeting and you have to be there.'

Boss to employee:
'I understand that you want time off for a dental check-up. However it is an important day tomorrow, as our new clients are coming, and I'd like you to be there. Could it wait till later in the week?'

Which of the above is likely to get the better result? In both examples, the second speech shows acknowledgment of the other's feelings and situation. Both child and employee respectively will feel they have been listened to. This kind of acceptance is

Paraphrasing

Paraphrasing, in the context of listening, is repeating back to the speaker what he has just said or giving him our interpretation or a summary of the speaker's message. It helps us clarify his message, and shows him we're listening. For example, if somebody yells, 'He never listens to anything I say!' we could respond with, 'You sound really annoyed,' and he will either agree or further explain what he feels.

Examples:

Tourist: 'I've just arrived on a flight from Dublin and my luggage has been sent to Bahrain!'

Hotel receptionist: 'Bahrain! That's disgraceful. You must be livid.'

Footballer: 'I've been training all week and I've pulled a hamstring, and I've got a match tomorrow.'

Fitness instructor: 'Seems like you've been overdoing it. I bet you're really disappointed.'

Such statements from the listener must be kept to a minimum. We should avoid taking over the conversation, but at the same time we want to keep it going. There is also a fine line here between being sympathetic and patronising. We need to find the correct tone in the above two statements so that we do not appear insincere. Paraphrasing occurs in situations involving directions or instructions. When we are receiving directions we often repeat them back to the speaker to make sure we've got the message.

Activity

Divide into pairs A and B. A gives B directions how to get from his house to college, including how to get to bus stops, stations etc. and B repeats back what she has heard. Then swap roles.

Tips for Effective Listening

- Remove or resist distractions
- Make sure you can hear properly
- Concentrate
- Focus on areas of interest and ask yourself, 'What am I getting out of this message?'

- Concentrate on the content and not the delivery
- Be patient and hear the full message before judging
- Give feedback
- Ask questions
- Keep an open mind – be objective
- Acknowledge the speaker and his/her emotional state
- Help to keep conversations going
- Thought is faster than speech so use the time to ask yourself internal questions and to challenge the message
- Observe body language and tone of speaker – there may be hidden messages!

Avoid:

- Fidgeting
- Frowning
- Looking at your watch

It is also important not to be too exaggerated or artificial in our listening responses. Inane nodding, staring or grinning will put the speaker off so a balance should be found. The skills mentioned should be tried and practiced and will depend on the speaker and the situation.

 # Note-taking

When we are faced with an hour-long talk or lecture on a new subject, hearing shouldn't be a problem, but understanding may be a challenge and retaining will be extremely difficult unless we take notes. Our memories are not capable of holding all the information given during the course of an hour, so a written record, to which we can refer later on, will help jog our memory.

Some suggestions:

- Always head the page with the date and subject
- Never try to copy entire sentences
- Listen for a few minutes and then summarise what has been said. Shorten everything – words by using abbreviations, sentences into keywords, phrases and headings
- Leave out examples, anecdotes and irrelevant information
- Stick to the facts

These will be rough notes and they need to be read and rewritten later in the same day. If they are left too late the memory wears thin and they will make less sense than on the day they were taken. Note-taking challenges us to use both our listening and writing skills. As we listen we distil the information and jot down what immediately seems important and relevant.

Activity

In pairs, take it in turns to read each other a detailed message (see sample messages below). In each case the listener should listen carefully to all the relevant information, and then relay the message back to the speaker to check for accuracy.

Sample Messages

Ms Williams, a company manager at Drumlinn Clothing Ltd., is returning from a trip to England on the 7.50 flight from Heathrow which is due to arrive in Dublin airport at 8.45. She was due to give a report to staff at a meeting on the company's end of year progress, scheduled for 11.00. However, the flight has been delayed and will not arrive now until 10.30. It will take at least two hours for her to get to the Drumlinn Clothing office, so the meeting has been rescheduled for 13.00. She wants Sheila to pick her up at the airport.

Get the 111 bus from outside the college to Dún Laoghaire station. Take a train to Tara Street station, get the 90 shuttle bus from Tara Street to Heuston Station. At Heuston, take the 10.30 train to Galway. Upon arrival in Galway at 14.15 go to the Island Ferries ticket office where you can buy your bus and boat tickets. Get the 15.30 bus to Rossaveal outside Kinlay House Hostel. This arrives in Rossaveal at 16.30 in time to meet the last boat, which leaves Rossaveal at 17.00 and arrives in Kilronan on Inismore at 17.45.

Activity

1. Make up your own messages related to your own vocational area.
2. In groups of three, A is the speaker, B is the listener and C, the observer. A relates a story or incident that happened to him. B listens using the listening techniques discussed and C takes notes on the techniques used by B. B then summarises what she heard. Swap roles so that each person plays each role once. Discuss how effective each was as listener and how the listening techniques aid communication.
3. Watch a video recording of a news item from television and summarise the main points. The radio could also be used for this activity.
4. Have someone in class read a passage from a book or a newspaper article. The rest of the students take notes from it, identifying the main topics and themes.

Chapter Review

1. Give a brief explanation of the importance of listening.
2. What is the difference between hearing and listening?
3. List six barriers to effective listening.
4. Explain the meanings of active and selective listening.
5. How can paraphrasing help listening?
6. List six points for effective listening.
7. Name four things that can help us to take notes.

Chapter 14 Speaking Skills

FETAC Assessment Requirements
Preparation for Message Giving, Dialogue, Discussion and
Negotiation, Oral Presentation

Topics Covered

The Voice

Language of Speech

Formal and Informal Speaking

 # The Voice

'It's the way you tell 'em!' This statement about telling jokes may seem trivial, but it rings true. Why is it that one person can tell a joke and it has the audience in fits of laughter, and then when we try to tell the same joke, word for word, it is met with an appalled silence? The reason probably lies in the way we use our voices. Many professionals take speech lessons to change the tone of their voices because they believe it will help their careers. A powerful deep voice can sound more convincing when giving a speech at a business conference than one that is high pitched or squeaky. The way we speak at an interview or during a speech can be more relevant to our success than what we actually *say*, so using the voice effectively is important in the study of speaking skills.

Discussion

Consider what types of voice makes people switch off. What teachers did you enjoy listening to in school and what ones did you not enjoy? Why?

Unlike writing, speech has a wonderful array of subtle variations that we use to alter the meaning of our messages. Of course these variations can lead to problems if we don't know how to use them properly but they enable us to liven up a word or phrase to give it depth, colour and meaning that is harder to recreate in writing. This is called *paralanguage*.

Pitch and Tone

Younger people have higher-pitched voices than older people. Sometimes when we are nervous, our pitch becomes higher due to constriction of the throat. We can help reduce this by relaxing the muscles in the stomach, chest, shoulders and neck. A monotonous voice is one that speaks in monotone – one tone – and is boring to listen to. Inflection is the changing of the voice's pitch and this is something we do naturally in speech often depending on our mood. The more we inflect the more interesting we can sound.

Volume

It is important that people can hear us when we speak. Some voices are naturally louder than others. A loud voice can be commanding and demands to be heard, but in some contexts a quiet firm voice can be more effective than a loud one.

Emphasis

We can illustrate the importance of specific words or phrases by placing emphasis upon them. We do this by changing the pitch and volume. Which words would you emphasise in the following sentences:

1. The next train for Galway leaves at 11.45 from platform number 3.
2. Don't you ever do that again!
3. Football is the most popular sport in the world today.
4. I will not tolerate this kind of behaviour.

Pace/Speed

We tend to speed up if we are excited, nervous or angry and we slow down when relaxed and comfortable or if we want to give emphasis. If we talk too quickly we can lose our listeners; if we are too slow we may bore them.

Articulation

When speaking we tend to contract words and sentences. 'What do you think?' becomes 'Whatcha think?' 'How are you?' becomes 'Howya?' 'Do not' becomes 'Don't' etc. It is easy to be lazy when speaking, especially in informal situations, and sometimes we just mumble and slur. We shouldn't be afraid to use our mouth, lips and tongue to full effect but without sounding forced or unnatural.

Activity

Try repeating some of these tongue twisters, focussing on articulation and pronunciation:

1. A big blue badly bleeding blister.
2. Rubber baby buggy bumpers.
3. A shifty snake selling snake skin slippers.

4. Eleven benevolent elephants.

5. Teaching ghosts to sing.

6. The big, black-backed bumblebee.

7. Selfish shellfish.

8. Really rural.

9. Unique New York.

10. The tip of the tongue, the lips, the teeth.

11. To titillate your tastebuds, we've got these tasty titbits.

12. Haemorrhoidal removal.

Activities

1. Give the Voice Expression

Sit in circles of five or six people. Take some of the phrases below and each person says the phrase using a different expression from the previous speaker. Try to express some of the following: neutral, asking a question (pitch goes up at the end), bored, angry, excited, scared, surprised, shy, happy, sad, whispering, shouting, crying, laughing, rapping, Gregorian chant, opera, sarcastic, proud, tired, suspicious, seductive. Try out different accents too.

  Suggested phrases:

• I want to go home

• It's my turn

• What are you doing tonight?

• We have to do an assignment

• The new computer's broken

• Hello, how are you?

• No one here gets out alive

• Drop it or else

• Just do as I say will you

• My helicopter is full of eels

• We've missed the bus

• This is getting ridiculous

2. Newscaster

Read aloud a short newspaper article and try to make it sound as interesting as you can. Depending on the nature of the news item you will have to adopt an appropriate tone of voice, e.g. serious, tragic, funny, quirky etc.

Newsreaders and comedians are helpful to listen to as they use vocal techniques to keep their audience's attention.

3. Choose one of the following passages and read it aloud, using appropriate voice expression:

Sorry? You're sorry? Is that all you can say? I've been waiting here for forty-five minutes in the freezing rain and all you can say is sorry. Why didn't you call me? You've got a mobile haven't you? Or did you forget that too? You know, sometimes I wonder why I bother with you at all.

Now there is a breakfast cereal to really get you going - 'Eat and Go'! If you're feeling slow and sluggish in the morning, flush away those early dreary blues with 'Eat and Go'! Full of natural goodness, iron and vitamins, 'Eat and Go' is made from organic oats and wheat, grown especially on our own farms and scientifically tested in our laboratories. Get yourself up and out with 'Eat and Go'!

It's the end of the millennium. An evil has been unleashed upon the world, an evil older than history. In a race against time, a struggle against the odds, a battle with forces too great for mere mortals, only one man knows how to stop the destruction of the entire planet. Arnold Schickelgruber is John Steel. Power beyond imagination, terror beyond belief. A film that will chill you to the bone.

Once upon a time, in a land far, far away, there lived a princess who was the most beautiful princess in all the land. She lived with her evil stepmother and two ugly sisters in a great big castle. One day, news went out across the land that a magnificent ball was to be given by the handsome Prince Charming to find a suitable princess for him to marry...

Language of Speech

The language of speech is very different from that of writing. It is far less formal and structured and grammar and punctuation often seem non-existent. We do, however, punctuate our speech with fillers such as 'well', 'you know', 'like' and 'em'. We hesitate, stammer, stop, restart, repeat and use redundant words. If we wrote down, word for word, what we said, it would look very inelegant compared to the written word.

Not all speech need be so chaotic. It depends on the context in which we are speaking. A conversation between friends would be very different from a prepared speech to a company board of directors. A well-prepared speech can be very close in structure and use of language to the written word.

Formal and Informal Speaking

Discussion

When the President of the European Commission, Romano Prodi, emerged from his car at the bottom of the steps of Government Buildings at the start of his Irish visit in 2001, Taoiseach, Bertie Ahern, shouted down to him, 'Romano, how are we doin'?' There followed hugs, handshakes, smiles and backslaps. For an official visit, many commentators saw this as being too informal. What do you think?

Informal speaking with friends and family is usually easy. We aren't under pressure to 'perform'. They will understand if we make mistakes, though we may occasionally feel a little foolish. Small talk, chit-chat and conversation are informal speaking activities we engage in everyday.

Formal speaking is more difficult. It needs to be more structured and grammatically correct and usually requires some planning and preparation. We use it in work situations, at interviews, giving talks and holding debates. Even giving someone instructions or directions needs to be clearly structured to avoid misunderstandings, which may lead to mistakes.

Here are some different types of speaking activities that are not too difficult and can prepare us for speaking assignments.

Narration

Tell a story to the class group. Here are some suggested topics:

1. Tell the story of your day up to the present moment. Begin: 'I woke up this morning...'
2. The story of a film/television programme/book you enjoyed
3. Describe what you did at the weekend
4. Describe a memorable holiday you went on
5. Tell a simple story (we all know fairy tales – better still, make one up!)
6. Tell a narrative-style joke

Try to make it personal, and include details to make it as interesting as possible. Use your voice effectively.

Description

1. Spend three minutes preparing a one-minute talk describing an activity with which you are familiar. Topics could range from your own pastimes, your work, sport, preparing a meal etc. Your tutor could give assistance in preparation. Your talk should result in your audience knowing roughly how to do the activity themselves.
2. Think of an everyday object/mechanical device/mode of transport etc. Describe it to the class group without revealing what it is. They should be able to work it out if your description is good enough.

Expressing Opinion

Many of us shy away from giving our opinion on some specific 'hot' topic. We may feel we cannot argue our point effectively enough to do so. Or we may simply not have any strong opinions about anything. Is this a good or a bad thing?

Activity

Here is a list of broad topics you might use either for a class debate or for practising solo speaking. They may be adapted as required. Consider the following before speaking:

1. Decide if you want to do some research on the topic beforehand
2. Decide on how you will approach the subject, e.g. an argument for or against, an informative or a persuasive speech etc.
3. What tone of delivery will you use? Angry, passionate, calm, reasonable etc.

- 'If I ran the country...'
- What I like/dislike about college
- Asylum Seekers
- The Internet
- Mass Media
- Young people drink too much
- Legalise Cannabis
- The Environment
- Global Warming
- Vegetarianism
- Advertising
- Religion
- Racism
- Mobile phones
- Television

Think up your own topics. There may be something specific to your own vocational area which you'd like to speak about.

Chapter Review

1. In what ways can we use our voices to improve our speaking skills?
2. Outline the differences between formal and informal speaking.

Dialogue Skills

Face-to-face interaction is the most direct, personal and open type of communication, because it involves verbal, non-verbal and visual contact. We can hear the speaker's voice, its tone, expression etc. and see his facial expressions and body movements. This can be an advantage or disadvantage depending on our viewpoint and the context. It is considered to be a healthy type of interaction because seeing the face and hearing the voice of someone we are communicating with is a human social need. Another benefit is the instant feedback from the receiver and the quick flow and exchange of thoughts, ideas and feelings. We can support what we say and can add expression and colour to our speech by using non-verbal signs. However, these can also reveal our emotions and personality, a good or a bad thing depending on what we want. Our accents can show our origins and our choice of words can reveal our level of education. So we cannot conceal ourselves easily in a face-to-face situation.

Successful interpersonal communication in a one-to-one or a group situation calls for a number of different skills, many if which are covered in earlier chapters of the book.
Here is a summary:

Perception
How we perceive someone can influence how we communicate with her. So:
• Avoid stereotyping and prejudice
• Make sure your observations of others are correct

Empathy

Understand where the other person comes from in terms of his beliefs, feelings, values and interests.

Acceptance

Communicate to others signs of recognition, acknowledgement and approval and respect any differences of culture, opinion etc.

Listening

Many conversations, discussions and arguments are ineffective because people fail to listen to the other person. If a speaker is not being listened to, there is no real communication taking place.

Speaking

It is crucial to be articulate and clear in what we say and to say what we mean.

Non-verbal Communication

Maintain appropriate eye contact and be in control of posture, gestures and facial expressions.

Controlling Responses

Effective interpersonal communication involves knowing when and how it is appropriate to respond and choosing appropriate responses to the situation. Avoid aggression and dominating a discussion; take turns in making contributions and beware of unnecessary interrupting.

Feedback

Give appropriate feedback and recognise and respond appropriately to feedback given.

Intent and Consent

Sometimes if we need to have a discussion with someone it is helpful to:
- State our intent
- Ask for consent

By stating our intent, we are preparing the receiver for our discussion and if she is prepared she will be in a better position to partake in and contribute to it.

By asking for someone's consent to have a discussion, he is more likely to oblige than if we dump him straight into the middle of it. We are also showing him respect by allowing him to decline our request if he wants. We shouldn't assume a person wants to, or has time to talk to us. Stating intent and asking consent invites co-operation and reduces the potential for misunderstandings.

Sometimes a simple, 'I need to talk to you, do you have a couple of minutes?' is a sufficient statement of intent and request for consent.

Negotiation Skills

Nelson Mandela once said, 'No problem is so intractable that it cannot be resolved through talk and negotiation rather than force and violence.' (*Trinity Today*, p. 17) He went on to say that, in negotiations, neither side is right or wrong, but all sides need to compromise.

We might think that negotiation is about business, but it is discussion between two people or groups of people when each wants something that the other might be unwilling to give. It is a process of finding compromise with each side gaining but also giving something.

Negotiation takes place when:

- An employee wants a wage increase
- A child wants to eat sweets and the parent wants her to eat vegetables
- A customer bargains for a better deal with a salesperson
- A couple has to decide who will drink and who will drive
- A band wants €10,000 to make a record and the record company offers €5,000.

Each side is usually out to get what it wants and this can result in distrust, suspicion, even anger and confrontation. We negotiate, because the alternative might be worse, e.g. workers' strike, break up of a relationship, a court case, even war. These alternatives are often used as negotiating tactics, e.g. 'If you don't give me what I want, I'll sue you.'

Guidelines for Negotiation
Pre-negotiation
1. Know your opposition's situation, skills, assets, strengths, weaknesses etc.
    (a) Be clear about your goals:
    (b) What are your initial demands?
    (c) What would you settle for?
    (d) What's your bottom line?
    (e) What do you both agree on?
2. If possible, choose a neutral space within which the negotiations can take place, where neither side feels at an advantage or disadvantage.
3. Timing – late in the day means some people may be tired and often irritable.

Discussion
The negotiations for the 1921 Anglo-Irish treaty between Britain and Ireland led by Michael Collins were held in Downing Street. How do you think this affected the parties?

During Negotiations
1. Aim for a win-win situation, where both sides leave reasonably satisfied.
2. Begin by asking for more than you think you will get.
3. Be prepared to compromise.
4. Never give ground without gaining something in return.
5. Don't put all your cards on the table at the outset, keep some in reserve.

Communication in Negotiation
1. Be clear and use plain language.
2. Clarify any possible ambiguities.
3. Keep a record of all proceedings especially any agreements.
4. Make sure both sides clearly understand the outcome.

Non-verbal Signs
Be aware of non-verbal *signs*:
1. Direct eye contact shows a firm positive attitude and willingness to communicate.
2. A warm facial expression shows interest and willingness to be persuaded.
3. A cold, steely-eyed, hard-faced expression can mean an inflexible attitude.

Lack of confidence is shown by:
1. Excessive smiling
2. Fidgeting
3. Hesitation
4. Speaking very quickly

Confidence is shown by:
1. Direct eye contact
2. Upright posture
3. Leaning forward slightly
4. Speaking slowly and deliberately

Negotiators should be flexible, firm, courteous, reasonable, persuasive, self-controlled, realistic and prepared to listen.

Breakdown

If a deal cannot be reached, one side might walk out. If there is a walkout, contact should be made immediately afterwards to prevent the proceedings from turning sour and to arrange another meeting.

Assessment Activities

1. Divide into groups of six. Conduct negotiations between management (three) and staff (three) of a company/organisation of your choice about proposed working hours and conditions over the Christmas period.
2. The following activities are for one-to-one negotiations:
   Two people, A and B are at a market and both see something they want to buy. A has enough money, B doesn't. B reminds A that she owes him money, the exact amount of the item for sale. They negotiate a deal.
3. You arrive at the station to catch the last train home, which is due to leave in five minutes. You suddenly realise you've lost your ticket and have no more money. Negotiate with the ticket collector to let you onto the train.
4. A rock star and her manager are arguing about how to leave the airport after a successful world tour. The fans are screaming outside and the manager wants them both to leave by a back exit but the star wants to meet the fans.
5. Granny is coming to stay. You have to give up your room but don't want to. Negotiate with your mother.
6. You want to buy a CD at a market stall, but it costs just a little bit more than the money you have on you. Negotiate with the stall holder.
7. The landlady wants to raise the rent. You cannot afford to pay what she is asking for. You'll only be there till the summer holidays and there are odd jobs you could do in the house. Negotiate a deal.

8. A famous TV presenter has missed his flight to London. He has to be there in time for the show later that evening. He tries to persuade a businessman, who wants to do some sight-seeing in London before a meeting the following day, to give him his seat.

Chapter Review

1. What communication skills are required for effective dialogue?
2. Explain the importance of intent and consent.
3. What is negotiation?
4. How can you achieve effective negotiation?

Chapter 16 The Interview

Interviews are primarily concerned with acquiring information about a person by means of a question and answer format. There are many types of interview, which we may experience in our college, working and social lives, such as a counselling or medical interview, or a progress interview in which an employer or tutor will assess our work and performance. This section will focus on the employment interview.

The primary function of an employment interview is for the employer to assess the potential employee. It also provides the candidate with an opportunity to learn about the position and the prospective employer and to see whether she might fit in comfortably or not.

What is of importance about an employment interview is that the employer gets to meet the potential employee face-to-face, to see and hear him first-hand. It illustrates the benefits of this kind of communication over all others. A letter, CV and photograph can only impart so much information. The interview fills in the gaps that they have left.

An employment interview is not always simply a one-to-one question and answer session. Nowadays, candidates may have to do a psychometric test (a series of rapid written questions, which determine a candidate's personality and ability), a role-play and may even find themselves at a group interview with a panel of up to five interviewers and a number of other candidates. It is well to find out beforehand what type of interview you will have.

Preparation

Pre-Interview

An interview for a job is likely to be a formal type of communication and, as such, we must be prepared for it. Here are some tips for interview preparation:

1. Be familiar with details in your CV and in your covering application letter.
2. It is vital to do some research on the organisation beforehand, e.g. the manager/owner's name, number of employees, products and services offered.
3. Do some research on the position for which you have applied, e.g. job requirements (what qualifications are needed), job specification (what duties and responsibilities it entails), if there is travel involved. Any research like this can impress the interviewer and show you are interested in the job.
4. Keep yourself informed and up-to-date on any recent developments in the job sector for which you are applying.
5. Prepare any relevant documents you think you might need to take with you, e.g. references, reports, portfolios, projects.
6. Think about what you are going to wear. It is best to dress formally avoiding bright colours, strong perfume or after-shave, or excessive jewellery. Clean clothes and hair are a must.
7. Prepare a list of your USPs (unique selling points), e.g. strengths, skills, experiences, qualifications, achievements, interests. These must be relevant to the job.
8. Be aware of your weaknesses and think of ways to turn them into positives.
9. Do a mock interview using the questions at the end of this section.

At the Interview

1. Be on time! Aim to arrive fifteen minutes before the time of the interview.
2. First impressions last, so try to appear friendly, polite and sincere.
3. Use appropriate non-verbal communication:
   - Shake hands firmly at the start and finish – the interviewer will usually offer her hand first.
   - Don't be afraid to smile.
   - Sit when asked. You may not be asked, so sit when it feels comfortable after the handshake, or just ask, 'May I sit down? Thank you.'
   - Keep a straight posture but not rigid and leaning slightly forward.
   - Don't cross legs, slouch or fidget.
   - Try to appear relaxed.
   - Maintain eye contact when speaking with interviewer.
4. Speak formally avoiding slang and fillers.
5. Don't use monosyllabic replies like 'Yes' and 'No'.
6. Give full answers but remember to stick to the point and avoid waffle.
7. Be honest. If you don't know an answer say, 'I'm sorry I don't know the answer to that.'
8. If you don't understand a question, ask to have it explained.

9. If the interviewer discovers any mistakes you've made or weaknesses you have, don't deny them.

10. Try to turn any weaknesses into positives, e.g. 'I've never done spreadsheets before, but I'm good at basic word-processing and I am quick to learn computer skills.'

11. Listen carefully to the questions and don't rush your answers. Take a second to pause and gather your thoughts.

12. Be positive and enthusiastic. You want this job, so try to show it!

13. Don't relax too much. Some interviewers use an over friendly tactic to catch candidates off guard.

14. Don't become defensive or argumentative if questioning becomes too rigorous.

15. Don't be afraid to sell yourself. Be confident but not cocky.

16. Never criticise a previous employer. It shows a lack of loyalty.

17. Have your own questions prepared in case you are asked if you have any.

18. At the end, thank the interviewer for seeing you and shake hands again.

19. The interview isn't over until you've left the room, so as you leave be polite, smile and don't bang the door.

After the Interview

An assessment and analysis of your performance afterwards is useful as preparation for future interviews.

List the questions you were asked. Evaluate the following:

1. Appearance
2. Entrance
3. NVC
4. Good answers
5. Bad answers
6. Listening
7. Your own questions
8. Details you forgot
9. Exit.

An interview, no matter what type it is, should be structured in a particular way so as to create a positive communication climate. This is largely up to the interviewer since she is the one who is leading the way, so to speak. However, interviewers can get tired, bored and nervous during long days of interviewing, so if you can create a positive climate by smiling and appearing warm and enthusiastic, it can be beneficial.

Interview Structure

There are three stages in an interview: the opening stage, the main body and the closing stage.

The Opening Stage

The opening stage in which an effective climate is briefly created by means of small talk or some sort of preview of what will be discussed. For example:

- 'I see you come from Galway. Do you like living there?'
- 'Since the last time you were with us are there any changes that have occurred in your life?' (If being interviewed for a job in the same organisation/company.)
- 'I see you went to Drumlinn College. Is Mr Maguire still teaching there?'
  Jobs can be gained or lost based on the first three minutes of an interview.

Main Body of Interview

This is where the main questions are asked and an interviewer often uses the funnel sequence of questioning, i.e. moving from broad topics to specific ones.

- Tell me about yourself.
- So, you're a good teamworker?
- Have you held any positions of responsibility?
- How would you deal with someone with whom you didn't get on?
- Tell me about a situation in which this happened?

The Closing Stage

The closing stage is also brief. You could be asked if you have any questions, there may be a short summary of the content of the interview, statement of a follow-up, e.g. 'We'll let you know...' and a friendly parting.

Formal or Informal

In highly formal interviews, both parties remain in their social and professional roles. So in an employment interview, the interviewer is the potential employer and the interviewee, the prospective employee. The interview will follow a standard format which the interviewer may have prepared and written out. Non-verbal signs from the interviewer like a firm handshake, formal dress, a formally decorated room and straight postures all communicate a formal style.

Informal interviews tend to be more relaxed, are less likely to follow a rigid structure, and the roles of the participants will be less clearly defined. Informal surroundings, casual dress and more in the way of chat, and smiling can signify an informal interview style, but are no less serious for that.

Types of Question

Open Questions

These allow the interviewee to expand and elaborate on certain topics. Examples:

- 'Tell me about yourself.'

- 'What sort of work experience do you have.'

The interviewee has the opportunity to steer the communication towards topics that will interest him or show him in a positive light.

Closed Questions

These call for a specific response, usually either 'yes' or 'no'.
- 'Did you enjoy your time at Drumlinn College?'
- 'How many modules did you take?'

They may be followed by open questions, e.g. 'What did you enjoy about it?'

Probing Questions

A probing question is one that tries to get beneath the surface to gain more information from an interviewee on a topic.

Interviewer: 'What did you enjoy about college?'

Interviewee: 'There was a good mixture of people there and it had a friendly atmosphere.'

Interviewer: 'What do you mean by a good mixture of people?'

Interviewee: 'There were people from different backgrounds, different nationalities, different ages and cultures.'

Interviewer: 'Why do you think that is a good thing?'

Interviewee: 'It helps to broaden your mind when you meet people from different walks of life. It makes it more interesting and stimulating. You begin to see that there is more to the world than simply your own way of looking at things.'

Hypothetical Questions

These kinds of questions give the candidate a hypothetical situation to see how he would deal with it. For example:

'Supposing you have a colleague who always arrives late and leaves early so that you are often left to cover for him/her. What would you do in this situation?'

Mirror Questions

Mirror questions reflect or bounce off the previous response.

For example:

Interviewer: Tell me about yourself.

Interviewee: I'm very interested in working with other people.

Interviewer: So you enjoy being part of a team?

Interviewee: Yes. I was involved in the Student Council at college.

Interviewer: Then you're interested in organising things with a group?

Interviewee: Yes. I think working as part of a group improved my communication skills.

In this way, interviewees have a degree of power over the direction of the interview.

Summary Questions

These generally cover topics that have already been discussed, or are intended to allow the interviewee to add anything of relevance that has been left out, e.g. 'Is there anything else you'd like to discuss?'

Leading and Discriminatory Questions

The following two types of questions are undesirable in an interview:

Leading Questions

These usually suggest a desired response and don't get an honest reply from the candidate.
For example, 'You wouldn't mind travelling as part of this job, would you?'

Discriminatory Questions

These are based on gender, marital status, race, religion and colour and are illegal as they may unfairly disadvantage the candidate. If asked such a question the interviewee may politely refuse to answer, e.g. 'I'm sorry. I would rather not answer that if you don't mind.'

Typical Interview Questions

Here is a list of typical interview questions:

General
- Tell me about yourself.
- What are your strong/weak points?
- What is your greatest quality?
- What are your greatest achievements?
- What have you done that illustrates initiative?
- How do you cope with stress?
- Can you work under pressure?
- What do you do in you your spare time?
- Do you read?

Education
- What did you like/dislike about college?
- Why did you go to college?
- How did you find the course?
- Are you satisfied with your results?
- Was there anyone you didn't get on with?
- Describe a problem you had to deal with at college.

Current Application

- What experience do you have for this particular job?
- Give me some reasons why I should employ you.
- Why would you like to work for this company?
- What attracted you to this job?
- What could you bring to this company?
- What skills or qualities do you have that would be useful for this job?
- What do you know about this company?
- How did you find out about this position?
- What are you looking for in a job?
- Where would you see yourself in five years' time?
- What kind of salary do you expect? (See below for questions about salary)

Previous Experience

- Have you held any positions of responsibility?
- What have you learned from any positions of responsibility?
- Have you ever worked as part of a team?
- How well did you fit into the team?
- Did you have to work with anyone who let down the team?
- How would you cope with a colleague you might find difficult to work with?
- Describe a problem you had to deal with in your last job.
- What were your main responsibilities at your last job?
- Why did you leave your last job?
- What did you like/dislike about your last position?
- What skills did you learn in your last job?

Do You Have Any Questions?

It is advisable to have a prepared question or two of your own as it shows you are interested in the job. Here are some suggested questions you may ask at an interview:

- Do you provide training?
- Are there opportunities for promotion?
- What sort of hours does this position entail?
- Do the employees get together socially?
- Do you have any plans to expand the company?
- Are there opportunities for working overtime?

Questions, either from the interviewer or interviewee, about salary always cause a little consternation. Many job advertisements include information about the salary, in which case there is no reason for the interviewee to ask, unless he feels the work is excessive for the amount being paid. An interviewee could ask, 'If offered this position, what would the rate of pay be?' Many people feel embarrassed asking this, so only ask if you feel comfortable doing so.

Assessment Activities

1. In pairs, interview each other as if for a job. Don't prepare the exact questions you will ask each other. At an interview we don't know exactly what we will be asked, so keep it as authentic as possible. Use the list of questions above as a guide. If possible bring in your CVs so that questions might be relevant to the interviewee.
2. For a more involved activity, put together an interview panel of around five students. The panel should prepare what kinds of questions each member will ask, e.g. one can introduce, another can focus on education, another on work experience etc. Conduct a number of interviews with volunteers and the rest of the group can assess the performance of each candidate.

Chapter Review

1. Outline the importance of non-verbal communication in an interview.
2. List five important points to be aware of.
3. List five things you should do to prepare for an interview.
4. List five things you should not do during an interview.
5. List five things to do after the interview. Why are these important?
6. Explain the meaning of open and closed questions.
7. What are leading and discriminatory questions and what is wrong with them?

Chapter 17 Groups and Meetings

FETAC Assessment Requirements
Dialogue Skills, Meetings, Business Documentation (Notice, Agenda, Minutes)

Topics Covered

Reasons for Joining Groups

Group Influence

Effective Group Communication

Synergy

Group Discussion

Meetings

Formal Roles

Documents for Meetings

Communication at Meetings

Conflict

Decision Making

We all belong to a variety of groups. From our families, through our colleagues at work or classmates at college, to our friends and members of clubs or societies, we are constantly involved with some form of group. Belonging to a group can have a positive effect on our wellbeing. We are, after all, highly social beings and regular interaction with others makes us feel socially 'connected' and this can contribute enormously in terms of life satisfaction. Being a member of a variety of groups helps us relate, interact and communicate with others and this interaction can improve our sense of social belonging as well as our self-confidence.

Interaction in a group is also a vital part of our working lives. Many employers look for people who can get along with their colleagues and work effectively as part of a group or team. If we can communicate well in group situations we will enhance our opportunities for employment and promotion.

Reasons for Joining Groups

Although we can often find ourselves in groups we didn't choose to join, for example our ethnic group, our family and our schooling, there are specific reasons why we join groups.

1. Security – we feel safe in the company of others who have the same interests
2. Identity – being a member of a particular group gives us a sense of who we are
3. Common Goal or Cause
4. Social Reasons
5. Information/Education

Group Influence

The groups to which we belong have a strong influence on how we think and behave. We are usually obliged to conform to the group's norms, i.e. patterns of thought and behaviour that is considered to be normal within a particular group. This may involve what we can and cannot speak about, the toleration of humour, an actual set of rules to which we must adhere or even wearing a specific type of clothing. These group norms are common to all members of the group, and help develop and build trust between members. Other groups who think and behave differently may be perceived as a challenge or threat. Our peer group often exerts peer pressure upon us to do things, with which we may not always feel comfortable.

Effective Group Communication

To make the most of our group situations we need to know how to interact with others successfully and how to make our groups effective in their tasks and to foster group cohesion. Dialogue and negotiation skills come into play in group situations, but there are a number of specific communication skills, which can help us contribute towards the groups to which we belong and maximise our benefits from them:

- Acceptance of other members and their ideas
- Offering support and praise to group members for their contributions, e.g. 'Well done', 'That's a good idea'
- Taking turns so that everyone can contribute
- Creating a relaxed atmosphere, using humour perhaps, without it becoming a distraction from the main purpose
- Showing agreement with other members
- Offering contributions, either by suggesting ideas or volunteering to take action

- Positive evaluation of others' ideas, e.g. 'That's a good idea, but it might work better if we...'
- Inviting the views and opinions of others, e.g. 'What do you think?'
- Bringing ideas together, e.g. 'Are we all agreed on that?'
- Suggesting actions, e.g. 'Why don't we...?'

Negative Group Communication

- Not contributing
- Insulting remarks about/to other members and their ideas
- Negative comments about the group's goals/purpose
- Regular disagreement with other members
- Behaviour that goes against what is acceptable to the group
- Self-centred communication
- Aggression
- Dominating behaviour

 # Synergy

Synergy, which comes from the Greek word 'sunergos', meaning working together, means that the combined effect of the whole of a group is more than the sum of its parts. In other words, a group works to its maximum effect if each member puts aside his/her individual interests in favour of the interests of the group. If we find our interests constantly clash with those of the group, maybe it's time for us to leave. If we don't actively contribute to the group, remain passive and silent, we become like a limb that has no purpose. The worst we can do is constantly be at odds with the group, in which case we may be asked to leave.

 # Group Discussion

Discussion in groups usually focuses on one or several specific aims or goals. It is important to keep the purpose of the discussion in mind, to keep from straying from the group's task and avoid red herrings. Discussions often get bogged down when one or two members concentrate and dwell for too long on minor and unimportant details. Discussions should move forward in the direction of a satisfactory outcome. Contributions to the discussion should:

1. Be relevant to the task at hand
2. Focus on the goal
3. Be constructive
4. Move the discussion forward

Meetings

Many people live in fear, and dread, of meetings. This is often because meetings involve lots of dry discussion, argument, boredom and sometimes very little in the way of progress and actual decision-making, the latter which should be one of the main reasons for meetings in the first place. Meetings are crucial to the smooth running of most organisations. Important decisions are made at every level of social and working life at meetings. In Government they are held to decide legislation or policy. Union meetings take place to discuss the welfare of the employees. A student council meeting may be held to arrange a social. At home when a family sits around informally to make plans for a holiday it is a meeting of sorts.

One reason meetings are held in such dread is that they are badly planned and poorly chaired. Meetings should be positive, constructive, stimulating and well organised. They can have many advantages. Within an organisation they can promote a sense of belonging, identity and involvement amongst members as each person is allowed to have an input. They can encourage a wide range of ideas and suggestions from the different participants. In short, they are democratic in that everyone can and should have an equal say.

Purpose of Meetings

1. Solving problems
2. Decision making
3. Negotiation
4. Generating ideas
5. Giving and receiving information

Types of Meeting

1. *Formal* – held according to specific rules and procedures, perhaps contained within a constitution
2. *Informal* – no specific rules
3. *Ordinary general meeting* – regularly held monthly or weekly to conduct routine discussion or business
4. *Extraordinary* – held outside the regular times to deal with a specific issue, often a crisis
5. *Committee* – a sub-group of the parent organisation
6. *Public* – any member of the public may attend, held in a public place, often dealing with political or community issues
7. *Private* – only members of the organisation may attend

Formal Roles

Chairperson

'Through the chair,' often precedes comments made at meetings. This means the chairperson is the 'channel' through which all comments and discussion are directed thereby ensuring that a certain degree of order is maintained and that any potential conflict is avoided, as participants do not communicate directly with each other. The most important person at a meeting is the chairperson. A meeting's success or otherwise can depend on how effectively it is chaired.

An Effective Chairperson

- Draws up the agenda with the secretary before the meeting
- Is impartial
- Has excellent communication skills
- Listens to all members
- Has qualities of tact, empathy and good judgment
- Maintains order without being dictatorial
- Encourages participation from everyone
- Sticks to the agenda
- Steers the discussion towards decision making
- Seeks consensus on decisions, by a vote if necessary
- Sums up main decisions/points ensuring that everyone clearly understands them

An Ineffective Chairperson

- Dominates the proceedings
- Loses control
- Allows private conversations and interruptions among the participants

The Secretary

The secretary is in charge of all written documentation connected with meetings. Before the meeting he should: send out notice of the meeting; draw up the agenda with the chairperson; prepare any documents, e.g. correspondence; prepare a suitable venue/room.

During the meeting: record attendance; read minutes of previous meeting; read correspondence; give a secretary's report if required; take notes for the minutes; support and assist the chairperson.

After the meeting he should: write up the minutes; deal with correspondence; take action on decisions that have been made.

The Treasurer

Basically the treasurer manages all finances and funds of the organisation and would give a treasurer's report if required, usually at an AGM.

Documents for Meetings

The Notice

Some meetings are held regularly on a specific day each month, for example, on the third Tuesday of each month; no notice is required, as members will be aware of this. However, if meetings are less regular the secretary should give notice, at least one week beforehand. It may be sent as a letter, memo, email or simply as a typed or handwritten notice on a notice board although each member should also receive an individual copy.

Sample Notice for Individual Member

Dear Member,

The next meeting of the Student Council will take place on Wednesday, 21 October at 1.15 in room 20.

Yours faithfully,

Caroline Stevens

Secretary

Sample Notice for Notice Board

Drumlinn College of Further Education
Student Council

The next meeting of the Student Council will take place on Wednesday, 21 October at 1.15 in room 20.

Caroline Stevens
Secretary

The Agenda

Often the notice will also contain the agenda, which is a list of all the items to be discussed at the meeting, giving participants time to prepare. The secretary and chairperson draw it up, though participants may request to have specific items included. Several items always appear on an agenda.

Sample Agenda

Drumlinn College of Further Education

Student Council

Agenda

1. Apologies for absence
2. Minutes of previous meeting
3. Matters arising from the minutes
4. Correspondence
5. Use of computer rooms
6. Next social
7. Any other business
8. Date of next meeting

Items 1 to 4, 7 and 8 above are almost always included. After the minutes are read (item 2) they should be approved (proposed and seconded) and accepted by the chairperson signing them. Item 3 is to allow members to discuss anything relating to what is read in the minutes, for example, to find out what action was taken since the previous meeting. Item 4 consists of any letters, memos or emails that the secretary has sent and received since the previous meeting. In order to save time these won't actually be read out in full unless the secretary is requested to do so. Item 7 is often abbreviated to AOB and gives members the chance to bring up any other topics for brief discussion.

Minutes

The minutes are a brief record of what was discussed and decided at a meeting written up by the secretary. They should be accurate and impartial. They should contain only the relevant points, but all motions and resolutions should be recorded word for word. They should be written in the past tense and record the name of the organisation, the date, time, venue and attendance.

Types of Minutes

Resolution Minutes record only the decisions or resolutions. All discussion prior to this is omitted.

Narrative Minutes record both discussion and resolutions. This requires good summarising skills, including only relevant discussion and leaving out unimportant details.

Action Minutes record a brief summary of the meeting and a column listing the names or initials of those responsible for implementing decisions made. These columns are important for recording who is responsible for what.

Sometimes the minutes will consist of a combination of all three.

Sample Minutes

Drumlinn College of Further Education
Student Council

Minutes of the meeting held on Wednesday, 21 October at 1.15 pm in room 20.

Present:
John Crowe (Chairperson)
Caroline Stevens (Secretary)
Orla O'Connell (Treasurer)
Neville Harding (Staff)
Sinéad Lombard
Joseph Onyesoh
Patricia McCarthy
Fiona O'Brien
Caitriona Connolly
Toki Tanaka
Fred Kenny
Stephen D'Arcy

Apologies: Joe Hayes, Kevin O'Shea, Sabina Meyer.

Minutes of previous meeting
The minutes of the meeting on Wednesday, 14 October were read, approved and signed.

Matters arising
The chairperson reported that he had met with the Principal and that a quotation for new lockers had been sought and that the lockers would be purchased in the new year.

Correspondence
The secretary read a letter from The Bayview Hotel offering student rates for the end-of-year social, and a letter from the Simon Community thanking the students for their fundraising activities. It was decided that a similar fundraiser will take place this year.

Use of Computer rooms
Patricia McCarthy expressed concern that students on her course did not have sufficient time in the computer rooms to work on assignments and that more hours should be made available to them from the computer department.

Toki Tanaka agreed and suggested that an extra hour each evening between 5 and 6 o'clock should be requested.

Next Social

Sinéad Lombard reported that she had confirmed the booking of Frankie's Nightclub for the next social, and that it was free of charge. Ticket prices were agreed at €3.50, and Joseph Onyesoh volunteered to design and print tickets.

AOB

Stephen D'Arcy said that a number of his classmates had complained about the canteen facilities. He said that the sandwiches were unsatisfactory and that hot food would be welcomed. There was broad agreement with his comments and Fiona O'Brien suggested that a canteen committee consisting of students, teaching staff and canteen staff be set up to discuss improvements. Neville Harding said that he would raise the issue at the next staff meeting.

The meeting closed at 1.50 and the next meeting was set for 4th November.

The timing and environment of meetings can often be factors that determine their success or failure. Most people are at their best around mid-morning, and slightly tired immediately after lunch. Many people with families to feed may find the hours between 5 and 7pm awkward. The size and arrangement of the meeting room is an important consideration and it is the secretary's job to ensure that it is suitable for the size of the group and that the layout will encourage, rather than inhibit communication. Here are some possible seating arrangements:

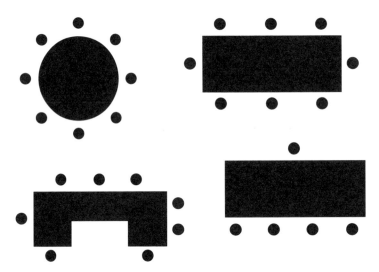

Fig. 17.1 Different seating arrangements.

Discussion

What are the advantages and disadvantage of these different seating arrangements?

Communication at Meetings

As soon as everyone has arrived and is seated, the chairperson will open the meeting with, 'I will now call the meeting to order...' or a similar phrase. The chairperson has the ability to set the tone by being firm but friendly. A word of greeting or welcome can often help in this regard. Once the routine items have been quickly dealt with, the first item should be introduced and the chairperson should address the whole group with a question like, 'What does anyone feel about...' or 'Does anyone have any suggestions for...'

Discussion is often dominated by a small number of participants who may intimidate new or shy members, and the chairperson should encourage everyone to contribute. A direct question here is useful, for example, 'What is your view on this matter, Fiona?'

For a newcomer it can be difficult to overcome the initial shyness, which prevents us from speaking. We may feel we have nothing to say, or that we are not as articulate as others are, or that we will appear foolish if we say the wrong thing. It is best to begin slowly and to gradually gain confidence with practice.

We must also be aware of non-verbal communication at meetings. We should make eye contact when speaking to people. If we avoid eye contact with someone he may think that we are ignoring him. We should try to keep a tone of voice that is positive, decisive and firm and doesn't become angry or aggressive. Our posture and gestures can all communicate a variety of messages. Interrupting is always tempting when in the thick of a heated debate, but we should hear someone out before giving our own views. Our choice of words should be such that we do not cause offence, e.g. negative evaluative statements like, 'That's a stupid comment.'

When speaking at a meeting we should begin by clearly signalling to the chairperson our intention to speak by raising our hand before the previous speaker has finished. If we hesitate the moment may be lost as topics are moved along quite quickly by the chairperson. We can start our contribution with a simple question: 'May I just ask what the previous speaker meant by...' or a simple comment: 'Through the chair, I agree with the previous speaker...' Only speak when it is relevant. We cannot know it is relevant unless we listen carefully to the discussion. As with other forms of communication we should be clear, concise and courteous.

The chairperson must determine that all aspects of a topic have been fully discussed before moving to a decision and that time is not wasted by spending too long on any one item.

Conflict

Conflict can be useful at meetings as it stimulates ideas and discussion, ensures that all perspectives are examined and increases members' understanding of opposing viewpoints.

Displaying effective and empathic listening techniques such as, 'I understand you feel strongly about this, but...' can help alleviate conflict. If a member becomes so unruly that the meeting cannot continue, a last resort may be to ask the member to leave or to abandon the meeting. When there is no conflict at all, it could mean that not all aspects of a particular subject have been explored, and as a result there may be a lack of thorough analysis.

Two types of group conflict have been identified: *disruptive conflict* and *constructive conflict*. Disruptive conflict is when members are: competitive, self-interested, adopt a win-lose approach, ignore opposing views, create an unhealthy communication climate which intimidates others, communicate defensively and resort to personal attacks. Constructive conflict occurs when participants are: co-operative, focus on the interests of the group, adopt a win-win approach, listen to opposing views, create an open and positive atmosphere and communicate supportively. From the outset, it is again up to the chairperson to set the tone for the meeting and if conflict does occur he must remain impartial and calm.

Decision Making

Consensus means that there is general agreement on a particular issue, and even if some people do not agree, for the sake of time or argument they agree to agree.

When the chairperson has judged an item to be sufficiently covered and a decision has to be reached, he may say, 'Do we have consensus on this point?' If there is no general agreement, a vote may need to be taken. In very formal meetings the chairperson will not allow any decision to be made without first having a *motion proposed* and *seconded*. A motion is a proposal to make a decision or take action about something. A motion must be proposed, seconded and start with the word 'that'. For example, 'I propose "that the next social will take place in Frankie's Night Club".' It is then followed by a vote, and if passed, becomes a *resolution*. These are the chief ways decisions are made at meetings.

Other Terms

Quorum – the minimum number of members required to attend a meeting in order for it to be valid.
Standing Orders – the written rules, which an organisation uses to run its meetings.
Point of Order – when a member checks to see if the proper procedure is being followed.
Amendment – a proposal to change a motion.

Assessment Activity

Hold a meeting in class. Begin by deciding on a scenario (see suggestions below). Elect a chairperson and secretary, and issue a formal notice and agenda to each member. If possible record on video or audiocassette, and afterwards watch/listen to the recording. Each member of the class should write up the minutes of the meeting as if she were the secretary.

Chapter Review

1. What are the advantages and disadvantages of group interaction?
2. List four ways of improving our group communication.
3. What is synergy?
4. What are purposes of meetings?
5. What are the duties and functions of a chairperson and a secretary?
6. Give explanations of notice, agenda and minutes.
7. Explain the two types of conflict.
8. What is consensus?
9. Explain how decisions are made at meetings.

Chapter 18 The Oral Presentation

There are a number of situations in which, at some stage in our lives, we may be asked to give a talk:
• Weddings
• Saying farewell to a colleague
• Acceptance of an award or prize
• Presentation of a new idea or product
• Introducing a guest speaker or new colleague at work
• Giving a talk to new colleagues, clients or students about our job
• Television or radio presentation

These vary from the very brief, informal chatty type talks, which require little preparation, to extensive, detailed and formal presentations that need careful planning and organisation. The latter is what is normally required of students for the purpose of a communications course.

Fear of Public Speaking

For most of us, getting up to give a talk before a group of people is a terrifying prospect. This is perfectly normal. Many professional speakers suffer from stage fright, be they actors, politicians, business people or teachers. One of the things about taking a communications course is that students often learn that they are better communicators than they had previously thought. If you have never given a speech before, you might automatically think you cannot do it. As a result of your self-perception, you have low self-esteem and you develop a fear of speaking. By learning the required skills, you can become confident and aware of your abilities and reduce apprehension.

An oral presentation is one form of speaking for which we can and *must* be well prepared. The better prepared we are, the better the talk and the less worries we will have. Let's first examine the problem of nerves that many of us suffer from.

The most common causes of anxiety are the following:
- The fear of communicating with people we don't know
- Not knowing our audience
- New or unusual situations
- Being the centre of attention, which makes us self-conscious and embarrassed if we appear awkward or say something foolish
- Evaluation – if we are being watched by a tutor or a video camera, we feel we are being examined
- Past failures in similar situations
- A learned anxiety from seeing others who are worried or afraid of giving a public talk
- Being badly organised and rehearsed.

Here are some suggestions for overcoming this type of anxiety:
- Remember that everyone gets nervous of public speaking, so you are not alone
- Concentrate on the task, i.e. the subject matter of the speech and not yourself
- It is impossible to give the perfect speech
- You will tend to notice your mistakes more than the audience, so don't be afraid of minor errors
- Conversation is full of minor errors and we tolerate those
- The main thing is to get the message across
- Visualise yourself as an effective public speaker: spend a few minutes each day leading up to the event, sitting quietly with eyes closed, and imagine yourself standing in front of the audience speaking clearly and confidently, the audience paying attention and applauding at the end
- Relaxation techniques: taking slow deep breaths before starting; swinging arms and rolling head and shoulders to ease tension.

It is virtually impossible to completely eliminate nerves before public speaking and it is also undesirable. A little anxiety is good, as it sharpens our concentration. Using some or all of the above exercises can help reduce nerves.

Extended Conversation

It has been said that public speaking is like an enlarged conversation, so we should try to speak as we do in a conversation. Most of us have little difficulty sitting around with a group of friends telling them what we did at the weekend. The major differences between the two are:

- A speech is better prepared
- There is no turn taking (questions from the audience come at the end)
- There are more listeners
- We are usually required to stand at one end of a room.

Like conversation, public speaking does not always have to be a formal type of communication. Often an audience will respond better to an informal, personal style, in which they will feel they are listening to a friend rather than being lectured to. Don't try to use language that doesn't come naturally but avoid using excessive slang. However, an audience will also expect a certain kind of performance, so we need to prepare it well beforehand.

 # Preparation

An effective presentation is the result of careful planning, preparation and rehearsing. Without adequate preparation the presentation will be ineffective and you will disappoint both yourself and your audience. It is a good opportunity to try something new, even if it is a daunting task, and many students of communications surprise themselves at the excellent results they achieve in this skill.

Choosing a Topic

If there is the option of choosing your own particular subject then choose a topic which is important to you. Talking about something you feel strongly about, or your own pastime or special interest will make a more effective speech. If you are interested in the subject, it is more likely that you can make it interesting for others. If you are required to speak on some aspect of your course, it gives you the chance to do some research into that area, or perhaps you have already researched it for a written assignment. Either way, whenever you are asked to give a talk, ask yourself the following questions:

1. Is it suitable material for an oral presentation?
2. Is it appropriate for the audience? Will they find it interesting?
3. Is it appropriate for the occasion?
4. Am I sufficiently interested in the topic?
5. Where can I get information on it?
6. Can I get some visual aids to make it more interesting?

Brainstorming

When you have chosen your topic, begin by brainstorming all the relevant themes associated with it, and create a mind map on a page. This will give you an idea of how large the subject matter is and you may need to narrow it down to one or two sub-topics.

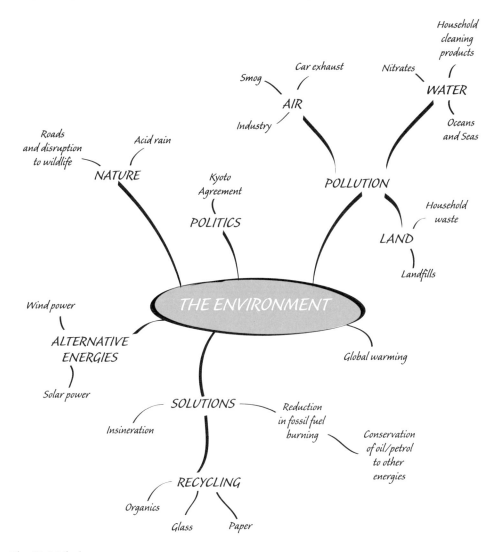

Fig. 18.1 Mind map.

Communication Objective

There are three main speaking purposes:

1. Entertainment
2. Information
3. Persuasion

Sometimes these three overlap. An informative speech can also be humorous and an entertaining or persuasive talk is also likely to be informative. Try to define into which category your speech will primarily fall. An entertaining speech is mainly to please and humour an audience. Be careful when using humour that it doesn't offend anyone, and jokes should be tested out in advance. A joke that doesn't work will cause severe embarrassment and ruin the speech. A speech that seeks to inform is mainly to increase the listeners' knowledge and awareness of a subject, to instruct them how to do something, to teach them a new skill or to train them in some new area. Persuasive speeches attempt to convince the listeners to do or think something, influence their attitudes or beliefs, inspire them to take action or sell them an idea or product.

Audience

It is important to know who your audience is going to be. Are they already interested in the subject? Do they have any prior knowledge of the topic? Will they share your sense of humour? Are they captive i.e. will they listen to your every word, or will it be a struggle to force them to pay attention? A good understanding of your audience beforehand will assist you in knowing what kind of talk you will give, and what sort of language and tone of voice you will use.

Next you need to define the specific aim of the speech for the audience. This is called the *main idea* of the presentation. Do you want them to take up tennis or join Amnesty International; do you want to show them how to grow their own vegetables, or how to paint; or do you want to have them rolling in the aisles? You should be able to summarise the main idea of the talk in one concise sentence. This may then be used as an opening statement and should be memorable even if the listeners don't remember the details of the speech.

 # Structure and Organisation

A well-organised speech can be a stimulating and inspiring piece of communication that will stay in our minds for some time afterwards. A disorganised presentation will be ineffective and even embarrassing. We have all experienced sitting in a class or listening to a speaker who rambles from one topic to the next, but do we remember what the main thrust of the speech was or any of the details? Probably not.

A well-organised speech works for the following reasons:
- It is easier to understand and digest
- It is easier to remember
- It has more impact and is more persuasive
- It increases the speaker's credibility.

A Well-organised Speaker
- Uses short sentences which are easy to follow
- Introduces the listeners to forthcoming information, e.g. 'The results of Global Warming are twofold:...'

- Gives information in a clear and logical way, e.g. 'Firstly...secondly...'
- Uses detailed statistical evidence to support information given
- Avoids vague and ambiguous information

Structure

There are three basic elements of an oral presentation:
1. Introduction – tell the audience what you are going to say.
2. Body – say it.
3. Conclusion – tell them what you've said.

Introduction

The opening of your speech is vital in that it can win or lose the audience. Remember that first impressions last, so try to get the listeners' attention from the start and explain briefly what the talk will be about. The introduction should have three sections:

(a) An opening statement that will get the audience's attention.

(b) A statement of the *main idea*.

(c) A rough outline of the main points to be covered.

1. For an effective opening, consider using one of the following:
    • A controversial statement
    • A quotation
    • An interesting statistic
    • A visual aid with impact
    • A rhetorical question
    • A personal experience or story
    • An anecdote
    • Humour (be wary of using a joke)

2. Next, state the *main idea* of your speech which should give the audience a good understanding of what it will be about. Here are some suggested openings, although you should try to be original:
    • Today I'm going to tell you about...
    • This presentation is to try to illustrate...
    • I want to inform you about...
    • This morning I'm going to show you how to...

3. The last part of the introduction should give the audience an outline of what it is you are going to tell them i.e. the main points briefly stated. This is called giving the audience 'signposts' which tell them where you are going. You might also let them know for how long you will be speaking and if you will be giving out notes.

Body of Presentation

A presentation for a communications course should be between five and ten minutes long, and should contain three to four main points. These can be selected from the mind map. They should be logically organised and they should flow smoothly from one topic to the next. It is important to try to link topics together, and signposts can be used for this purpose. These can be single words, phrases or whole sentences. It is crucial to let the audience know when you are moving on to a new point. If you jump from one topic to the next too abruptly, the audience may get confused and lose interest.

Typical signposts might include the following:

- Firstly, secondly, thirdly...
- Due to this, because of this, as a result of this, consequently...
- Therefore, and so...
- Finally...
- Now that we've seen how the internal combustion engine works...
- I've looked at the causes of insomnia, now lets have a look at the effects...
  Non-verbal signposts can also be used:
- The fingers can indicate first, second and third points
- Silence or a pause can let the audience know that we are moving on to a new topic
- Visual aids can be used to introduce a new point
- Intonation is a good way of showing that you have reached the end of one section of your talk.

Conclusion

An effective conclusion is vital so as to finish on a strong note that will leave a lasting impression on the audience. At all costs avoid trailing off limply at the end. A conclusion is often like the introduction in reverse. Use it to summarise the main points and to leave the audience with a final thought on the subject that they will hopefully remember. Don't be afraid to repeat information at the end of the talk. The audience cannot rewind to go back over the topics already stated, so it is useful to restate some of the key ones, especially the main idea. As with the introduction, it should be brief and no new themes should be introduced at this stage.

Typical concluding statements:

- I hope you now have a better grasp of...
- Let me leave you with one final thought...
- Today I've given you a brief outline about...
- I hope I have succeeded in informing you about...

 # Delivery

There are four possible types of delivery:

1. Impromptu

An impromptu delivery is usually given without any preparation whatsoever, is short and off the cuff and is unsuitable for a course presentation. These are given at informal gatherings, welcome or farewell presentations.

2. Off by Heart

Learning it off by heart can be very time consuming, hard work and it may end up like a recital and not a talk. Unless you have a great memory and are a natural performer, this type of delivery should be avoided.

3. Written Speech

Reading from a written speech can sound very boring, as it is a different type of communication - a reading not a talk. You have little opportunity to make eye contact with the audience, and your voice can be lost as it disappears into the page.

4. Cue Cards

These are prepared cards with notes written on them to which you can refer every few minutes. This is ideal as you can develop the ideas on the cue cards and still maintain sufficient eye contact with the audience. It is the method most professional speakers use.

Cue cards are small blank cards that can be easily held in the hand during delivery of the presentation. They should be numbered and notes should be kept brief - ideally keywords, or short phrases. Only write on one side of each card.

Before writing out notes on your cue cards, write an outline of the speech. This might seem like a waste of time but it gives you the opportunity to go through each point carefully, and to make sure that it is properly structured. Each topic and/or section should be headed appropriately, making references to any support material you might want to include at various stages (see below). The outline is a way of stitching together each piece of research and signpost, introduction, body and conclusion into a coherent whole. From this you can then practise by reading through it a few times to get used to the flow of the material, and then by selecting keywords and phrases to write on your cue cards. These will act as notes and prompts for the presentation itself.

NVC

Appropriate non-verbal communication can make the difference between an attentive audience and a bored one. An audience responds to a speaker's body language. If the body language displays signs of interest and enthusiasm for the subject, mainly by facial expression, but also by gestures and posture, the audience will respond in the same way. If you show that you are disinterested or bored, the audience will feel the same. There are a number of points to consider:

The Voice

The voice is obviously crucial in an oral presentation. The following are the main points to consider:
1. *Volume:* you must be audible and loud enough so that the people at the back can hear. Practise projecting your voice to someone at the opposite end of a classroom.
2. *Tone and pitch:* you should aim to make it sound interesting by sounding interested. Otherwise, it may sound flat and monotonous. Inflection, changing the pitch of the voice so that is goes up

and down, adds interest to a speech. We do this naturally when we speak about something that interests us. When we are nervous, unfortunately, we tend to remain at one level. Practise changing the pitch of your voice at different parts of your presentation.

3. *Emphasis:* try to put stress on words that need emphasising.
4. *Pause:* pausing is effective and useful to let the audience take in an important point, to signal a change of topic and to give yourself a break to check your notes. Don't be afraid to pause briefly every now and again.
5. *Speed:* we speed up when nervous. If you're too fast you may lose the audience; too slow and you'll bore them.

In all of the above, aim for variety as this will make it sound interesting and hold the audience's attention.

Posture

Studies have shown that an audience and listeners pay more attention to a speaker who has a straight posture. We don't have to be unnaturally rigid, but if we have a comfortably straight spine and neck, the audience will take us more seriously than if we slouch or have our hands shoved deep into our pockets.

Avoid:
1. Shifting balance from one foot to the other
2. Staying rooted to one spot
3. Walking around too much
4. Putting your back or shoulder to audience

Gestures

Appropriate and controlled hand gestures can help support a speech. Unanimated speakers can be boring to watch, but don't use exaggerated gestures that will distract the audience.

Avoid:
1. Folding arms
2. Hands in pockets
3. Hands behind back
4. Wringing hands
5. Rattling keys/coins in pockets
6. Fiddling with hair, pens, glasses etc.

Facial Expression

Introducing yourself with a smile can win over an audience from the start, and an occasional and appropriate smile during the talk can keep them on your side. The eyebrows are a very expressive part of the face and we can emphasis a point by raising them.

Eye Contact

Ideally we should make eye contact at least once with everyone in the audience. But by staring at one person we can make him feel uncomfortable. By looking at the back wall, out of the window or at the floor, it appears that we are communicating with these things and not with the audience.

Venue

You should find out about the venue beforehand. What sort of equipment is available? Is the room big or small? Will your voice reach those sitting at the back? Will there be a podium or somewhere to put your cue cards and/visual? If you don't know the venue beforehand you might be surprised to find yourself somewhere totally unsuited to your needs.

Support Material

A presentation that involves just speaking can be quite dull, so support material can help to make it more stimulating. Any of the following will add evidence, interest and credibility:

- Statistics
- Comparisons
- Quotations
- Visual Aids
- Anecdotes/stories

Visual Aids

Visual aids support and enhance an oral presentation in the following ways:

1. They make a talk interesting and stimulating.
2. They have a strong and lasting impact.
3. They can help an audience understand the topic by:
   - illustrating with examples
   - simplifying and supporting verbal information with charts or graphs.

Types of Visual Aid

- Models and objects
- Maps
- Diagrams
- Charts and graphs
- Drawings, paintings, sketches
- Photographs
- Posters

Handouts are also useful as support material.

Means of Display

Audio-visual Equipment:

1. *Overhead projector* – It is relatively simple to photocopy an image onto acetate or a transparency, which can be used easily on an overhead projector.
2. *Slide Projector* – can be expensive
3. *Video Recordings* – It is often possible to find a relevant video clip to accompany the talk. We might even decide to make one if we have access to a camcorder. Here are some useful points to remember:
   (a) Don't let the video dominate – if you try to compete with a television screen you will lose every time! A maximum of about two minutes in length.
   (b) Don't talk over the video unless it has no soundtrack. Preferably introduce it and explain what the audience will see, and give a brief analysis afterwards.
4. *Audio Recordings* (strictly speaking not a visual aid but will add interest)
5. *Power Point* – this is a technology that uses a computer to create text and images for projection onto a screen. It will depend on availability.
6. *CD-ROM* – dependent on availability.

Audio-visual equipment needs to be well prepared and rehearsed in advance and can often be expensive.

Other Visual Aids

1. Whiteboard
2. Blackboard
3. Flip Chart

These are not usually prepared beforehand, but you need to have clear handwriting or drawing skills.

Handouts

Don't make your audience read too much. They will forget about you! It is best to use these at the end of the presentation.

General Points to Remember about Visual Aids

1. Keep them simple – simple language, simple images, limit the amount of text you use - an audience doesn't like to read too much.
2. Make them big – they should be visible at the back of the room.
3. Make them relevant – use visuals only if they support and enhance the speech. Don't let them dominate.
4. They should look good – no one likes to look at unattractive or messy images.
5. Colour is more attractive than black and white.
6. For a five to ten minute talk, three to five visuals are sufficient.

Effective Use

1. Prepare them well in advance of the presentation.
2. Plan exactly when to use them during the talk. Don't have them all at the beginning or all at the end.
3. Practise using them.
4. Check that any equipment is working.
5. Don't block the audience's view of them.
6. When finished using them, switch them off or remove them.
7. Remember, technology can always let you down at the last moment, and you may have to speak without it.

Font Sizes

If using written text, make sure you use appropriate sized words. Here are some guidelines:

Flip Charts/Blackboards/Whiteboards	
Headings	3 inches
Sub-headings	2 inches

Computer Printouts		
	Acetates/Transparencies	Handouts
Headings	36 point	18 point
Sub-headings	24 point	14 point
Main Body of Text	18 point	12 point

Dealing with Questions

When you've finished speaking, there is still the question and answer session to deal with. There may be an applause at the end. Then it is up to you to invite the audience to ask any questions they might have. It may take a few seconds before someone plucks up the courage to ask, so be prepared to wait. Here are some hints:

- Listen to the question carefully
- Repeat the whole question in case not everyone has heard it
- When answering, address the whole audience, not just the questioner
- Give answers that are complete, concise and to the point
- When finished answering, ask the questioner if your reply was sufficiently clear
- If you don't know the answer, don't 'wing it'. Be honest and say you'll have to look into it
- Stay alert
- Bring the question session to an *effective* conclusion, e.g. 'If there are no further questions…'
- Say thank you at the end

Finally

Preparation for an oral presentation requires sufficient practice. This means spending time rehearsing either in front of a class group, at home with friends or family or on your own in front of a mirror. Without practice you will be ineffective. Each time you practise, you improve.

Practice is vital for the following reasons:

- To time the speech to ensure you won't go too much over or under the allotted time
- To get used to the layout of and the flow of words in the speech
- To practice using the cue cards, and filling out the keywords and phrases
- To get comfortable with your visual aids, if using any, and to know when to use them
- To improve your overall performance: voice, body language, eye contact etc.
- To get completely acquainted with and confident of your subject matter

Activity

Read some of these famous speeches:

1. 'I Have a Dream' by Martin Luther King Jr, 28 August 1963:
   http://www.mecca.org/~crights/dream.html
2. Irish Proclamation of Independence, 24 April 1916:
   http://www.iol.ie/~dluby/proclaim.htm
3. The Gettysburg address by President Abraham Lincoln, 19 Novemver 1863:
   www.saxton.com.au/lincoln.html
4. Former South African President Nelson Mandela Inauguration Address, 10 May 1994:
   http://www.saxton.com.au/Mandela.html
5. Former US American President John F Kennedy Berlin Address:
   http://www.saxton.com.au/Kennedy.html
6. English Prime Minister Tony Blair to The Dáil, 26 November 1998:
   http://www.stanfordplus.com/education/inspirationals/blair1998.php

 # Chapter Review

1. Explain the main causes of fear of public speaking.
2. How can we get over our fear of public speaking?
3. What are the similarities and differences between an oral presentation and a conversation?
4. How can you organise a speech to make it easy for an audience to understand?
5. Why is it important to structure a speech?
6. What are the advantages of using visual aids?
7. Describe effective ways of opening a speech.
8. What are the disadvantages of a speech that is read out or learned off by heart?
9. How can you make effective use of visual aids?
10. Explain the importance of NVC in an oral presentation.
11. Outline how to deal with questions from the audience.

Part 6

Communication
Technology

Chapter 19 The Telephone

Discussion

The videophone has never made it into the mainstream market as the telephone has, in spite of a number of attempts. With improved technology it may be here soon. How would this change the way we speak long distance to others? How does communication by telephone differ from face-to-face interaction? What are the advantages and disadvantages of not being able to see (or be seen by) the person at the other end of the line?

The telephone network is one of the most rapidly developing technologies of recent years with new services, products and providers appearing almost daily. Deregulation of the telephone market has led to the arrival of new companies such as ESAT to compete with Eircom, thus creating a drive for better and cheaper services. Fibre optic cable has meant that more information can be sent faster down the line.

Mobile Phones

It has been said that the mobile telephone is the most successful new communication medium ever seen. Mobile phone use has seen remarkable growth since the nineties. In the five years between 1995 and 2000, the number of mobile users in Europe increased from less then 3 million to over 60 million. Mobile calls now account for over half of all telephone use.

Discussion

1. Most people seem to have a mobile these days. What are they mainly used for? Could we still do the following with landline telephones?
   - Chat
   - Business
   - Making appointments/arrangements
   - Have fun
   - Information
   - Keeping tabs on children
   - Games
2. Consider the following questions:
   (a) What are the advantages of mobiles over landline phones?
   (b) Who really benefits from them?
   (c) What about people whose work involves being mobile, e.g. couriers, plumbers, builders and electricians?
   (d) Could mobiles change or benefit the way we work in any way?
   (e) Is it really an advantage to be contactable all the time?
   (f) How does it adversely affect our social lives, e.g. if we are out with one friend and talking to another on the phone.
   (g) Is it too easy to call someone to change/cancel an arrangement?
   (h) Does this make us too casual and uncommitted in our personal relationships?

Mobile Etiquette

Apart from irritating ring tones and overhearing other people's conversations, the one aspect of mobile etiquette is knowing when to switch them off. Make a list of places and situations where mobiles should be switched off.

Text Messaging

Since making voice calls on a mobile is still relatively expensive, many people choose slightly cheaper option of using SMS (Short Message Service). This has been a hugely popular way of communicating in recent years especially amongst younger users. In Europe, over 1 billion messages are sent every month. It is a useful medium of communication for:

1. Short messages
2. When the receiver is too busy for a full conversation, unavailable or travelling
3. Storing a message for later reference
4. Saving money especially when calling abroad
5. Simply keeping in touch
6. Deaf people to keep in contact

Typing in words on such a small keypad can be laborious, and we don't like to waste time, so a whole new form of writing has developed using a combination of abbreviations and numbers. Here are some examples:

Anyone – ne1	One, won – 1
Are you ok – ruok	See you later – cul8r
At – @	Someone – sum1
Before – b4	Thanks – thnx
Can – cn	Today – 2day
Excellent – xlnt	Tomorrow – 2moro
For, four, fore – 4	Tonight – 2nite
Forward – fwd	Want to – wan2
Great – gr8	

While this kind of language can be useful for quick informal exchanges, there is a danger that it might be mistakenly slipped into formal communication contexts such as letters of application, reports and college assignments.

Another feature of SMS technology is predictive text, which anticipates what words the user is trying to key in from the first few letters. The benefits in time saving are obvious but there are concerns that abbreviated and predictive text are eroding literacy as rules of grammar, spelling and punctuation are being avoided or ignored. Text messaging might even be changing the way we write, but for the moment we should aim to be aware of the differences and use each style in its appropriate place.

Another concern about text messaging is stalking and bullying. Many schoolchildren now have mobile phones and some are becoming victims of bullying, with threats and abuse being sent to them via text. Harassment is another problem that some people have experienced. If somebody gets hold of our number without our knowledge, he may pester us with messages of a sexual nature. Students have also been known to use text messaging during exams.

 # Health Risks

There has been much debate regarding the potential health threat due to radiation from mobile phones. The manufacturers usually say that their research shows no correlation between mobile phone use and damage to human health. However, hundreds of independent studies show a possible link between mobile use and cancer, anxiety, increased blood pressure, sleep loss and heating of the brain. The debate is still going on, but expert advice is to err on the side of caution and follow these tips:

1. Keep mobile calls short – no longer than fifteen to twenty minutes at a time.
2. Young people should use them only for essential purposes.
3. Employers who require employees to use mobiles should make them aware of the risks.
4. Consider the SAR (Specific Absorption Rate – amount of radiation the body is exposed to during mobile use) when buying a new mobile.
5. Avoid use while driving.

Wireless Application Protocol (WAP)

Mobile access to the Internet sounds like a great idea but at the time of writing it hasn't really taken off. The predictions are that as soon as the technology improves, more people will access the Internet with their mobiles than with their computers. The next generation of mobile technology – G3 (3rd Generation) – could see us: talking 'face-to-face'; shopping; surfing the web; checking news and weather; and finding a restaurant all from our mobiles.

Telephone Technique

New technologies and gadgets aside, it is important to be able to use the telephone effectively as a medium of voice communication especially in the workplace. A lot of time and money can be wasted when a telephone call is badly made, and often business can be lost due to poor telephone technique.

Customers must be impressed, and a telephone call may be their first impression of an organisation/company. Improving our telephone skills and manners is simple and can help us avoid some of the more common mistakes.

A number of simple rules apply:

1. Speak clearly – phone line quality can vary greatly due to the different types of phone in use today. Many people, unconsciously or not, adopt a 'telephone voice', speaking more slowly, politely and neutralising their accent in order to be clear.
2. Be prepared – be clear in your mind what you want to say and how you want to say it.
3. Make notes of the information you need to give and receive.
4. Have pen and paper handy.
5. Keep records of calls – in case you make two calls to the same person by mistake.
6. Pave the way for further contact – there may be new and unexpected developments, or simply more business to be done.
7. Be patient.
8. Use good manners at all times.

9. Use an appropriate tone of voice.
10. Try to be as efficient as possible, avoiding delays.
11. Apologise for any delays.
12. Empathise with the caller.

Discussion

Answering Calls
1. In many European countries, people answer the phone by stating their surnames. How practical is this?
2. There are many ways of answering the telephone. Here are some of the standards:
   - 'Hello.' (This can range in tone from friendly to abrupt)
   - 'Hello, Drumlinn College of Further Education, Orla speaking.'
   - 'Drumlinn College of Further Education, Orla speaking, how can I help you?'
   - 'Drumlinn College of Further Education, good morning.'
   - '631907.'

Discuss the pros and cons of each of the above and its suitability in social and vocational contexts.

Placing Calls
Standard opening lines when making calls are as follows:
- 'Hello, may I speak to Mr O'Reilly please?'
- 'Is Karen there?'
- 'Hello, my name is Joe Dunne, is Alan there please?'
- 'I was wondering if I could speak to Simon.'
- 'Hi, I was looking for Sharon Wallace.'

Discuss the pros and cons of each of the above and its suitability in social and vocational contexts.

Remember that when using the telephone, the person at the other end cannot see our non-verbal signals, so we should remember to be aware of the tone and pitch of our voice. Try to sound friendly and interested.

Leaving/Taking Messages

If the person we want to speak with is unavailable, it is appropriate to ask to speak to someone else who may be able to help, or we may be asked to leave a message. Usually we will be asked for our name and number and we will be contacted later on. However, messages can go astray, or are taken down incorrectly. It is advisable to find out who is taking the message. This acts as a kind of guarantee that it will be passed on. Depending on the type of call, it may be more courteous to call again especially if we require the information or are selling something. In this case we can find out when the person will be available for us to call again.

When taking a call, if the person asked for is unavailable we should find out if anyone else can help. If not, the following information should be taken down:

1. Caller's name
2. Caller's number
3. Name of the company/organisation (if there is one)
4. Reason for the call i.e. the message
5. Date and time of the call

It is important to *repeat this information* back to the caller. It only takes a minute and is worth it to prevent mistakes. Sometimes there are phone message slips, which are simple to fill out. A caller should never be left on hold for too long without frequent voice contact, or she may wonder if she has been cut off, or forgotten about. If she has been waiting for a few minutes, we can give her the option of whether she wants to continue to hold or leave a message.

Sample Phone Message Slip

Message for _____

Telephone Message _____

_____

_____

Caller _____

Of _____

Number _____

Time received _____

Date _____

Message _____

Message taken by_____

Redundant Information

As we have already seen, spoken messages can be full of fillers and information that is unnecessary, so we need to differentiate between what is necessary and what is redundant.

Activity

Have someone read out the following message. The rest of the group should extract and take down the essential information:

'Hi...em...my name is John O'Rourke and was interested...It's 3.30 on Tuesday 15th and I want to find out about the job advertised in the *Evening Herald* last Thursday...the...aah...tenth, I think...I'm pretty qualified for the job as I've got a certificate in web design and I'm quite easy going. If you could call me, my number is 07-2375664. I will be here till about 5.30 this evening or you can reach me on my mobile after that at 086-8845396, but I tend to go to bed at about 11.30, so not after then. If I don't hear from you I'll call again in the morning.'

Answering Machines and Voice Mail

Many of us are still terrified of leaving messages on a machine, and yet they are now a regular part of daily communication, both socially and vocationally. One reason we find them so disconcerting is that there is no feedback and we feel we are speaking into a vacuum. It is therefore well worth preparing a message in case the person we want isn't there. Mostly people will say they'll call you back if you leave a message. If not, it can be useful to leave a brief detail about the nature of the call. Remember, wait for the beep and always leave the following:

1. Your name
2. Your number
3. Date
4. Time
5. A short message

Assessment Activity

The tutor should provide an instruction sheet for one of the following:

1. Ballyduff Fitness Centre
2. Dr Sheerin's Surgery
3. The Concert Hall Booking Office
4. Kilmurphy Theatre
5. Glenfane Tourist Office

e.g. an advertisement for a concert/play/surgery hours/opening hours with dates and times, and a corresponding pre-recorded answer phone message on an audio cassette giving some changes to the dates. The students then listen to the message individually and leave their own message with requirements (making an appointment, booking tickets, making enquiries etc.) on another cassette.

Alternatively, the students write out an answer phone message for one of the above (or an organisation related to the vocational area), stating that the place is closed, but that the caller can leave a message. Sitting back to back, each person will then 'call' another, listen to the answer phone message being read out and leave a message with all the relevant details and requirements. Then swap roles. Record the messages onto audiocassette.

Fax

A fax machine is really a long distance photocopier that can send copies of documents electronically via the telephone line to another machine anywhere in the world. It is likely to be replaced eventually by email attachments (see chapter 22), but for the moment it is still in use. Dial the receiver's fax number, insert the document and it feeds through, sending a copy to the receiver for the price of a phone call. Sometimes a cover sheet is sent with the message. It usually includes details such as the sender's name, receiver's name, date, subject heading and whether it is a routine or an urgent message.

Further Activities

If the facilities are available, make some real phone calls. Here are some suggestions:
1. Make an enquiry (e.g. travel times and costs)
2. Make an appointment (dentist, doctor)
3. Make a reservation or cancellation
4. Make a complaint or apology
5. Make a date
6. Offer congratulations or sympathy
7. Enquire about a service (plumbing, window-cleaning)

Chapter Review

1. Explain the recent changes in the telephone system and how they will influence our lives.
2. What are the advantages and disadvantages of text messaging?
3. What precautions should we take to avoid health risks associated with mobile phones?
4. What information needs to be recorded when taking a phone message?
5. What five pieces of information need to be left on a telephone answering machine?
6. What is a suitable way of answering the telephone in a vocational (formal) situation?
7. List five rules for effective telephone technique.

Chapter 20 Computers

A computer is a 'machine that performs tasks, such as mathematical calculations or electronic communication, under the control of a set of instructions called a program.' (Microsoft Encarta '98)

 # History of Computing

In 1943, the founder of IBM, Thomas Watson, reckoned that there was a world market for about five computers. How wrong he was! Computers have changed and are continuing to change the way we live our lives. In today's high tech world hardly anyone can have remained untouched and uninfluenced by computer technology. In fact it is hard to imagine a world without computers, yet, only thirty years ago they were still relatively new.

As early as the seventeenth century machines were being invented to do mathematical calculations, but the idea of a machine that could efficiently store and retrieve information goes back to the 1940s. There are four stages in computing history:

1. 1940s–50s – Development of mainframe computers, which fill entire rooms, require closely monitored humidity and temperature and are used by large corporations. The transistor, invented in 1948, acted as an electric switch and had a huge impact on the design of computers.

2. 1950s–60s – The development of the silicon chip, which contains tiny electrical components, greatly increased the power and speed of mainframes. The microchip continues to shrink in size and enables manufacturers to produce smaller and cheaper computers. Supercomputers, the largest and fastest computers, were developed and are mainly used for scientific applications in the chemical, motor and aeronautic industries, and by the military. The computer on Apollo 13 had less power than one of today's Nintendo games machines.

3. 1970s – Microcomputers (e.g. personal computers) were smaller and easier to use. Video displays (screens) were added and they had more efficient storage devices and greater computational abilities. 1980s - Personal Computers (PCs) became widespread, can be used by almost anyone and are found in homes and offices the world over. They replaced typewriters, calculators, and manual accounting techniques and are used for storing files and records and for word-processing. Laptops are portable PCs.
4. c. 2003 – Picocomputers are smaller, more powerful and, it is predicted, will become much more widespread than PCs. They will be automatically connected to the Internet, have voice recognition and be capable of accessing far more information than current devices for example anything from our exam results to the contents of our fridge. There are a variety of picocomputers that include palmtops, set-top boxes, videophone watches, electronic checkbooks and embedded devices found in many everyday appliances. The experts predict that they will eventually be embedded into walls of buildings and clothing.

Hardware and Software

A computer consists of hardware and software:
Hardware – the physical components such as the keyboard, mouse, visual display (screen), modem, printers and all the electronic circuitry inside the computer, disks, chips etc.
Software – the instructions given to computers to enable them to perform tasks, often using programming languages.

Computer Uses

People use computers in ways they may not even realise. In business, computers use bar codes and scanners to check customers' credit, to check out goods at a supermarket, and check warehouse supplies. EFT (Electronic Fund Transfer) electronically moves funds in the form of wages and bills between bank accounts. Minute computers are embedded in many household electric appliances such as thermostats to control heating, security systems, clocks, radios, microwave cookers, videocassette recorders and stereos. Cars use computers to regulate the flow of fuel. Computers are used to control traffic lights, hospital equipment, to book flights, to fly aircraft and design anything from buildings to birthday cards. Most organisations use them to keep files on accounts and personnel. At schools and colleges they assist in writing reports and assignments and designing posters. Educational software can be used to teach subjects in a new and entertaining way.

Computer technology is changing so rapidly that it is difficult to predict with any real accuracy what they will be doing in a year's time, let alone five. What we can say with certainty is that they are getting faster, smaller, cheaper, more efficient and easier to use every year. Artificial intelligence is an idea that has tantalised computer experts for years, and some believe that computers which will have their own independent thoughts, are not too far away.

Discussion

Are we becoming too dependent on computer technology? Are computers replacing people at work? Do computers make our lives any better? Could we live without them? What is the potential impact of a future that is even more computer dominated than today? What are the advantages and disadvantages of living in the Computer Age.

Data Protection

Data is the name given to the type of information processed by computers. Since computers can now store vast quantities of data, laws have been passed to ensure that information of a sensitive or personal nature is used only for the purpose for which it is intended. For example, at work, files are kept on employees, which might contain personal information on their health, ethnic group, political beliefs, sexual orientation, criminal convictions, family circumstances as well as details of their absences from work, salary, accidents and discipline.

Under the Data Protection Act 1988, computer users with such personal information must register with the Data Protection Commissioner. Institutions that may have such information include banks, insurance companies, marketing companies, public authorities and public sector bodies such as health boards, county councils, schools and colleges.

Under the act:

1. An individual has the right of access to the information about him on request.
2. Data should be collected and maintained lawfully and kept accurate and up to date.
3. Data should not be changed or destroyed.
4. It should be kept safe and secure and be accessible only to authorised staff members.
5. Unspecified or unlawful disclosure of such information is not permitted without the individual's consent. (Sometimes marketing companies place an individual's personal details on another company's mailing list and that company will use it to advertise by sending junk mail.)
6. Data should be maintained only for as long as it is relevant. For example, if an employee leaves a position, the employer should delete the information on that individual.

Data may be disclosed if it:

1. Assists in a criminal investigation
2. Prevents injury, loss or damage to others or their property
3. Assists in investigation of money owed to the state
4. Is requested by the individual

An offence against the Act can result in a fine of up to €63,500. An individual may request a copy of any data relating to him or ask that it be updated, or deleted. Grievances against suspected abuse of the Act can be made to the Data protection Commissioner.

See also The Freedom of Information Act 1998 in chapter 23.

Chapter Review

1. List seven everyday uses of computer technology.
2. What is EFT?
3. Outline the main points of the Data Protection Act. Why is it important?

Chapter 21 The Internet

The Internet is an **inter**national **net**work that links computers from all over the world and allows information to travel from one to another. It has been described as the most important technological development for humans since the industrial revolution. It is impossible to be accurate with statistics about Internet use, as they are increasing all the time, but at the time of writing there are over 400 million people using the Internet worldwide and over 40% of them are from America and Canada. In Ireland more than one million people use it at home. Compared to other communications media, the Internet has grown far more quickly to become a mainstream medium. Radio took 37 years to reach 50 million listeners. Television took 15 years to reach the same number of viewers. The World Wide Web took just 3 years to reach the same number of users. The Internet gives us access to vast amounts of information that is constantly being updated and expanded to make it faster and more efficient.

Origins

In 1957, when the Soviet Union launched the first satellite, Sputnik, the US became concerned that the Soviets were winning the space race. As a response they set up an agency called Advanced Research Project Agency (ARPA) to explore and develop military, space and communications projects. When NASA took over the space programme in 1958, ARPA concentrated solely on military research and computer technology.

ARPA set about developing a system that could share information and resources between individual computers. It was basically an institution for the military and university academics. A key concept was that there should be free and easy access to knowledge, ideas and information. It therefore developed a sense of community and shared knowledge so that any user anywhere could build upon and improve the system. ARPAnet was born when two American universities connected their computer systems via the telephone network. Unfortunately, the first attempt resulted with a system crash! In the 1970s email became one of the most popular applications. It turned out that people just liked to communicate with each other!

The World Wide Web was set up in 1989 by Tim Berners-Lee. The Web is not the same as the Internet, but an application of the Internet that makes it easy for anybody to navigate their way around it. Essentially it means that there is a common computer language that links all the different documents on the Internet, and we can easily jump from one to another without having to learn the language. The Web has transformed the Internet from being a tool for academics and researchers to a global media phenomenon.

Getting Connected

It is possible to go online without actually owning a computer. Internet facilities are available through the following:
- In public places such as airports and train stations
- Internet cafés
- WAP phones
- Web television
- At work
- At college.

However, to be a home user we need the following:
* Computer
* Modem – this connects the computer to the telephone wall socket via a cable
* Phone line
* Service provider

Most people use their own telephone line for the Internet, but there are other options and newer technologies that are just around the corner. Here are three of them:

ISDN

Integrated Services Digital Network is a digital phone line, which is more expensive than a normal phone line but it also means faster access.

Cable

With cable TV it is possible to access the Internet using a cable modem. The benefit of this system is that it is faster than the phone line, and there is no need to dial up to go online. One drawback is that if everyone else on our street has it, then the speed of access will decrease.

DSL

Digital Subscriber Line uses the phone line but is faster and once installed is always connected. It is already available in the US, but at the time of writing hasn't yet reached Europe.

Internet Service Provider

Internet Service Providers are locally based companies with high-speed computers that are permanently linked to the Internet. An individual working from home dials up the ISP via the modem and phone line and is then routed to the Internet by the ISP's computer. The cost is the cost of the local call to the ISP. Some companies set up a Local Area Network (LAN) which may be confined to a building or an office. It connects all the computers in that small area. A Wide Area Network (WAN) can connect computers over greater geographical distances, for example, a company's regional offices. The biggest WAN is the Internet itself.

 # Using the Internet

The Internet was originally designed as a tool for research. Today it is still used for research and study by school children, college students and academics the world over. As such it is an invaluable resource. It is also much more.

Here are some of the reasons people use the Internet:

1. News – online newspapers, e.g. *The Irish Times* and the *Irish Independent* can be read online. News sites and Newsgroups. Newsgroups often provide cutting edge stories right from the source, unfiltered by corporate media companies and newspaper editors.

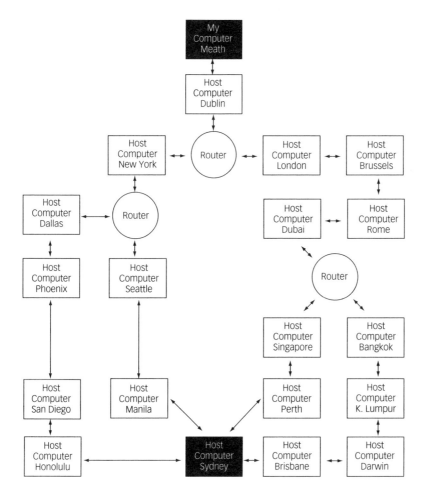

Fig. 21.1 Diagram of Internet showing computers connected to each other and ISPs etc.

2. Shopping – some supermarkets enable us to buy our groceries online and have them delivered. Online shops like Amazon and Indigo will sell almost anything, if we have a credit card, and deliver by post.
3. Online banking – most services are possible, unless we want actual cash immediately.
4. Postal services
5. Entertainment – online games, online radio, music downloads, cinema releases, video clips, books, reviews, humour, buying concert tickets.
6. Holidays – checking destinations, exchange rates, booking flights and accommodation.
7. Discussions and chat.
8. Exchanging email.
9. Sending and receiving documents and photographs.
10. Visiting online art galleries.

11. Checking sports fixtures and results.
12. E-business – online marketing, correspondence, getting customer feedback.
13. E-learning – online courses.
14. Professional advice – legal, medical, financial etc.

Due to its enormity, the task of actually locating the precise information we want can be daunting and frustrating. Some say the Internet is like a vast library, but a highly disorganised one without a proper system of classification. There are a several ways of retrieving information from the Internet:

 # The Browser

The Browser is the vital piece of Internet software that acts as a window through which we can explore its contents. Today a browser includes a whole range of facilities and services such as email that enables us to get maximum use of the Internet. Most new computers come with a browser already installed. Netscape Navigator and Internet Explorer are the two most popular browsers used today.

When we are set up and ready to go online for the first time, we can click on the browser icon on the desktop, which will open the homepage of our ISP or the browser's homepage. A *homepage* is the first page that appears on the screen and also refers to the first page of any *website*. A *web page* is a page of information that appears on the screen and a *website* is a collection of web pages on a specific subject. By moving the mouse around a page we notice that the arrow becomes a hand on certain words and phrases, usually coloured blue. These are *hyperlinks* to other web pages and sites and by clicking on the mouse when the hand appears, new pages will appear on the screen. This is what is called *surfing*, jumping around from page to page and site to site, exploring the vast amount of information available to us.

Each web page has an address called a *URL* (Uniform Resource Locator). If we know the precise address we can key this into the address box at the top of the screen and press the return key. The browser will locate the page and open it for us. URLs are case sensitive, in other words, the address has to be *precisely* keyed in, paying particular attention to capital letters and punctuation. If we insert one wrong letter or punctuation point the page will not appear.

A URL, like *http://www.ireland.com* usually consists of four parts:

1. The protocol, http (HyperText Transfer Protocol), is the set of rules and standards which enables web pages to be displayed and transferred. When keying in a URL we don't need to include this.
2. www stands for World Wide Web and we usually need to type this in.
3. The host name, in this case, ireland. This is the name of the company or organisation and is called the *domain name*. (*www.ireland.com* is the URL of *The Irish Times* website)
4. .com which tells us that it is a commercial organisation or a company

This ending is called an *extension*, and there are many different types of extension, which give us information about the site. Here are some typical extensions:

- .org – a non-commercial organisation
- .net – a company dealing with networks, like *www.eircom.net*

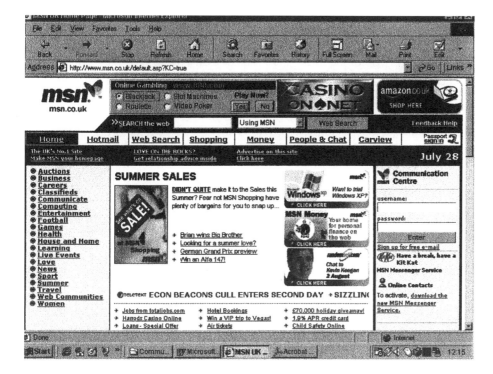

Fig. 21.2 MSN Browser.

- .edu – an American educational establishment
- .gov – an American governmental department or institution
- .ie – an Irish website
- .co.uk – a company in the UK
- .de – a German site.

Above the page is a toolbar with a number of buttons or icons to help navigate the web. Depending on which browser we are using these will vary. Typical ones are:

- *Back* – enables us to return to any of the pages we have already visited
- *Forward* – having gone back, we can also go forward to whichever page we previously visited
- *Stop* – this button stops downloading the current page, useful if it is taking a long time
- *Refresh/Reload* – this will reload the page again if it didn't load properly the first time
- *Home* – takes us back to the homepage
- *Search* – enables us to search the Internet for specific topics (see below for more)
- *Favourites/Bookmarks* – If we want to have easy access to a site we particularly like we can store it in a list of favourite sites/pages
- *History* – this shows which sites we've visited
- *Full Screen* – enlarges the page to fill up the screen
- *Mail* – takes us to our mail server
- *Print* – allows us to print pages from the Internet
- *Edit* – this enables us to create and edit web pages

Searching

In order to maximise our use of the Internet we should know how to find the information we require without wasting time. Click on the *Search* button on the toolbar. The screen splits into two and a *search engine* appears on the left with a box where we can type in keywords of the topic of interest. Type in a keyword and click *Search* or press the return key on the keyboard. A list of sites or 'hits' appears on the left-hand side, and if we click on any of these, the pages will be displayed on the right. The disadvantage of this is that the screen becomes too cluttered.

Search Engines and Directories

If we don't have the exact address of a website the best way of finding information is via a *search engine* or a *search directory*. One of the best search directories is Yahoo.

Enter *www.yahoo.com* in the address box. The Yahoo homepage will appear with lists of categories to choose from. Click on a category and gradually narrow down the search. For example, if we want to find information about music in Ireland and we don't know the address of any particular sites we can begin by clicking on 'Regional', then 'Countries', 'Ireland', 'Entertainment', 'Music' and so on until we narrow it down to the specific information we require. At the very top of the screen are details about how we got to the particular site.

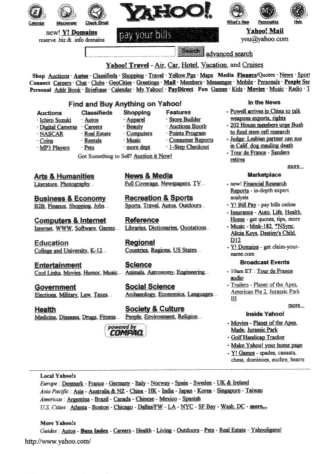

Fig. 21.3 Yahoo homepage.

Search Engines

Here is a list of some of the most popular search engines currently used:

* Altavista   *www.altavista.com*
* Ask Jeeves   *www.askjeeves.com*
* Dogpile   *www.dogpile.com*
* Excite   *www.excite.com*
* Google   *www.google.com*
* Go To   *www.goto.com*
* Infoseek   *www.infoseek.com*
* Look Smart   *www.looksmart.com*
* Lycos   *www.lycos.com*
* Mamma   *www.mamma.com*
* Northern Lights *www.northernlights.com*
* Webcrawler   *www.webcrawler.com*

Each search engine has its advantages and disadvantages and it is important to remember that if we don't find what we want with one search engine, we can always try another. This is because search engines don't all contain the same sites. Each search engine has a help page, which provides useful information about how to use them efficiently. When the search engine homepage appears just type in a keyword that is based on the category of the subject required, and click on search or press the return key. However, if we type in the keyword 'music', for example, a list of sites will appear on the screen, which could run in to thousands, even millions. Then we have to scroll down the list clicking on the sites we think might be useful until we find what we want. This can be very laborious not to mention time consuming. In order to avoid this we need to be more specific with our keywords. So, instead of 'music', we should type in the genre, or type of music we want. Again we have to be careful with our choice of keyword. If we type in 'country' we may get a list of geography or travel sites. Even if we key in 'country music' the search engine could come up with sites relating to either countries or music and not necessarily country music. So we need to enter the phrase in quotation marks, 'country music'.

When we find we have gone down a dead end in our search, we can always click on the *Back* button to retrace our path.

Activity

If the facilities are available, search the Internet for information on one or two of the following:
* Jobs in Ireland
* Cinema listings
* Train timetables
* The latest home news
* Health risks of mobile phones

Validity of Information

Once you have found the information you need, it is important to question its validity. How reliable is it? Is it true, factual or just somebody's opinion? The Internet is such that anybody with the right know-how can put up a website and there is no overall controlling body to check the material. As a result there is a lot of rubbish out there!

There are a few ways of determining whether the information we find is reliable or not. If a site contains any of the following it is likely to be sound enough:

1. Author's name indicating that there is nothing to hide
2. Contact number or address
3. Information that is well written, with good punctuation and spelling, and it appears that time and effort have gone into creating it
4. Author's qualifications showing that they are an expert in the particular field which they are writing about
5. References to other texts on the topic indicating that research has been carried out

The URL will also tell us about the author's allegiances, for example, if it ends in .com it is a commercial organisation and may want to sell us something. There can be many different sites for the same organisation so the official website might be more reliable than an unofficial one.

Advertising on the web has also become unavoidable. On almost any site we visit we will see banner advertising at the top of the web page, often with a flashing sign saying 'Click Here'. Don't. Although these ads may be annoying, they mean that most of the information on the web is free, since they provide revenue for the websites. It doesn't take long to distinguish between what is information and what is advertising.

Printing, Saving, Copying

Printing Web Pages

Reading pages on the web from the screen can become quite tiring, so when we find a page that we would like to read properly, we can easily print it out. We simply click on the *Print* button or icon on the toolbar and the page will print. However, occasionally we find that they don't print out exactly as they are on the screen, as screen sizes and paper sizes don't always match. It is also important to remember that when we print a web page, everything, text and graphics, might be printed. In some cases only text will print. Moving images won't of course come out. We should also note that a web page may contain a huge number of pages and if we click print, the whole document will print out. To print a selection from a web page, we can highlight the section of text we want, click on *File*, select *Print* and choose the selection from the print range. Alternatively, we can *Copy* and *Paste* the text onto a Word file and print it from that.

Saving Web Pages

We can also save a web page or site onto a floppy disk or hard drive simply by clicking *Save As* on the File Menu, and saving it on to whatever disk we want. Then in future we can access the exact page without going online.

Copying Information on a Web Page

If we want to copy a section of a web page, we can highlight the specific information by clicking on the mouse and holding our finger down on it and dragging it across the section we require. Click *Edit* on the toolbar, click *Copy*, open a document, click Edit and *Paste*. It will appear on the document. To copy an image, click the right hand side of the mouse with the cursor over the image, a box will appear, click on *Copy*, and complete the process as above.

Favourites/Bookmarks

If we come across a website we would like to visit regularly we can add it to our favourites or bookmark, depending on which browser we are using. Simply open the page or site, click on *Favourites* or *Bookmark* click on *Add*. This creates a shortcut to that site.

Interactivity

The Internet would be very dull if it wasn't for the millions of people who use it as a communication tool everyday. It is a place for people to: meet, keep in touch with friends and relatives, to exchange opinions and views on a variety of topics, to 'chat' and even to start relationships that can end up in marriage!

One of the main differences between traditional forms of media and the Internet is that most mass media are 'top down' and communication is largely one-way. In other words, the messages are sent from a producer, editor, director etc. to the public. The Internet, because it has no central control or 'producer', is thought of as being 'bottom up', in that anyone, once online and with the required skills, can send out information. This is why the Internet is regarded as a revolutionary medium. Many see it as a truly democratic and empowering forum in which anybody can help shape and influence what it becomes.

There are many ways of being interactive on the web. Here are the main ones that we are likely to come across:

Chat Rooms

These are highly popular types of Internet interactivity. They were created because people wanted to communicate in 'real time' and not have to wait hours or days for email replies. Many websites have chat rooms, which are provided for free and we can choose from a wide range of categories to talk about depending on our tastes and interests. When we register for a chat room we are asked to give an identity name or number or a combination of both. It is advisable not to give real names, as we can never know for sure with whom we are communicating. It might be our next door neighbour!

While chat rooms can be fun and a novel way of meeting and communicating with people, there are problems associated with them. The anonymity surrounding them means we never really know whom we are chatting to and young people are especially vulnerable to being misled. Frequently chat room conversation becomes sexual in nature and therefore children should be supervised when using them.

There have been some benefits associated with chat rooms. Many schools set up links with other schools for the purpose of chatting and forging links. In Northern Ireland, schools of different religious denominations found it very useful as the children found they could communicate openly regardless of their background and without any threat. In the chat room everyone is equal. Chat rooms can also be useful for people who are naturally shy and who would find it difficult to start a conversation under normal circumstances. They often find it easier to communicate with others when they cannot be seen or heard. In this sense, the chat room can be liberating for people who feel restricted by their appearance or their voice. It is well to remember, however, that we tend to communicate very differently online to when we are with someone face-to-face. We lose our inhibitions and self disclose with people we have only just met. Communication moves very quickly on the Internet and normal social rules do not always apply. Soon we feel we know someone intimately and feel we can tell them whatever we want, only to find out later that we have been deceived.

In many of the world's industrialised nations, the traditional community in which people once lived, shopped, worked, met and interacted has crumbled and in its place a virtual community is growing. However this community is not as 'real' as the old one and we can pretend we are someone completely different online in order to gain acceptance.

Discussion

What are the differences between having an online group discussion and having a real group discussion?

Guest books

When we visit tourist attractions we are often asked to sign a guest book to give our opinions or comments. It's the same for websites. Normally the interaction is one-way and we would only receive an automatic reply. They are used, as in the real world, for website owners to gauge the reactions of visitors to their site and these responses are usually put up for other visitors to read.

Email Links

When visiting a site, we may see an email link which, when clicked, opens an email message box with the site's email address filled in. So the visitor can simply email the site to ask for information or leave comment.

Discussion Boards

Many sites like to encourage visitors to discuss topics associated with the site. This is good for the site, as it attracts people to return to the site and therefore help sell advertising, and it can also benefit the visitor who can share views and gain new information with other visitors interested in the same topic.

Newsgroups

Newsgroups are similar to discussion boards except they are located on ISPs. Newsgroup articles on pretty much every conceivable topic, from aardvarks to zymurgy, can be accessed via the browser or email, which usually has a newsgroup reader program built in. We can read messages or articles, reply, post our own questions or messages and make contact with people all over the world who share our interests. However, we must always remember that for every expert on a subject, there is a nutcase, who will use newsgroups just to rant and rave. It is advisable to read about the newsgroup before posting a message. There are fairly strict guidelines about what is and isn't permissible. Usually advertising and insults are not allowed. (See Netiquette in chapter 22)

Voice Chat/Internet Telephone

This is a relatively new development in Internet technology, which involves literal online chat. With a microphone, headset, the relevant software and a sound card we can talk to people on the other side of the world, for the price of a local phone call!

Video-conferencing

To avoid travelling long distances to go to company board meetings, video conferencing allows people to partake in 'virtual meetings'. By means of cameras and microphones, participants can sit at home in front of their computers and see and hear the other people who may be sitting at home thousands of miles away.

Causes for Concern

With the arrival of every new form of media, there come concerns about dangers to individuals and society. With the Internet there are perhaps even more concerns since there are no ways to control it and it is wide open for all kinds of criminal and nefarious activities.

Security

Anyone, using a computer today needs to be aware of viruses. Basically, a virus is a program that can cause damage to a computer system. Before the Internet came along, viruses were spread mainly by floppy disks transferring files from one computer to another. Over the Internet viruses can be transmitted by email attachments and by downloading files and programs. Most modern computers come with a virus-checking program that should be used to check any email attachments after they've been saved to a floppy disk. Some anti-virus programs update automatically, if not they should be upgraded every month or so as new viruses appear almost daily. The positive side of this is that anti-virus software companies are constantly checking for new viruses and creating ways of detection, prevention and cure.

We should also take care when giving information about ourselves over the Internet, especially personal details like addresses and telephone numbers. When joining groups on the web, we are often asked for such details. At best it will only result in junk mail, electronic or real. At worst we could end up being stalked. Many people are still cautious about giving credit card details over the net. When shopping online, most e-tailers provide secure sites that cannot be seen by a third party, so credit card numbers can only be viewed by the buyer and seller. Some experts believe it is actually safer than giving details over the telephone.

 # Hacking and Cracking

Hacking is the illegal art of breaking and entering someone's computer system. Most hackers are concerned with breaching the computer system of large companies and governments to impress their peers. The reward is prestige and seldom financial, although many who are caught are subsequently employed by companies to mend their security systems!

Crackers are hackers who do it to either make money from it or with some particular reason in mind, such as causing damage to the system. Ironically they also serve the purpose of exposing security flaws to the companies who have been hacked!

 # Regulation

Should it be legal to spread racist messages across the Internet? This kind of question raises a major debate on whether the Internet should be subject to censorship or to permit unlimited freedom of expression. In many countries the Internet is censored. In Myanmar (formerly Burma) it is banned, and in China and Malaysia it is illegal to put anything on the Net that criticises the governments in those countries. Regulation is clearly a problem for a medium that crosses all national boundaries. In many countries where freedom of expression is highly valued, any attempt to restrict information on the Internet is seen as being contrary to the Universal Declaration of Human Rights.

The Global Internet Liberty Campaign is an organisation concerned with matters of human rights, civil liberty and personal freedom and it refers to Article 19 of the Declaration. It states that everyone has the right to 'freedom to hold opinions without interference and to seek, receive and impart information and ideas through any media'.

The Internet is regarded by many as an ideal forum for the free expression of ideas and opinions no matter what they are and any restriction on that goes against such liberties. However, not all material is suitable for children, for example, pornography is huge on the Internet because there is a market for it. In most western countries it is legal to view pornography in the privacy of one's own home. However, this means that children, even while harmlessly surfing, can accidentally stumble across pornographic sites. A misplaced full stop in a URL could inadvertently open up the wrong website. The unlimited access to any type of information, one of the positive aspects of the Internet, is also one of its biggest problems.

Child pornography, on the other hand is contrary to the International Convention of the Rights of Children, and in Ireland, the Child Trafficking and Pornography Act 1998 makes it illegal for anyone to produce, distribute, print, publish, import, export, sell, show or possess any child pornography.

The Internet has provided paedophiles with a new means for them to commit their crimes. They enter chat rooms posing as children, 'talk' to children, arrange to meet them, or set up servers from their own computers and publish and distribute material to other paedophiles. Such activities are difficult to trace but cyber crime units are being established by police forces all over the world to try and prevent such activities. Organisations such as the Movement against Paedophilia on the Internet are also helping to raise awareness and tackle this problem. In recent years, a number of paedophile rings have been infiltrated and the criminals brought to justice. The Wonderland Club was one such ring. However, many can still go undetected and it is still a major problem.

In 1997, a Department of Justice, Equality and Law Reform working group was set up to investigate some of these issues. It produced a report, 'Illegal and Harmful use of the Internet' which stated the following illegal uses of the net:

1. Actions which cause injury to children, e.g. child pornography, child trafficking
2. Actions which cause injury to human dignity, e.g. incitement to racial hatred
3. Illegal gambling
4. Infringements of privacy and intellectual property rights, e.g. publishing someone's music or written work on the net without permission
5. Libel – defamation of character
6. Threats to economic security, information security and national security

The report recommended a system of self regulation by Internet service providers and would include:

1. A national public hotline to report illegal use of the Internet
2. An Advisory Board bringing together the partners needed to ensure successful self-regulation
3. The introduction of appropriate awareness measures in schools and colleges etc.

Internet Service Providers in Ireland have now set up a hotline to try to eliminate child pornography from the Internet. Members of the public can report sites of this nature to the hotline

– *www.hotline.ie* – and the Internet Advisory Board has been established and includes members of the Gardaí, the Film Censor's Office, the Child Studies Unit of University College Cork and the children's charity, Barnardo's.

The first attempt at an international treaty regarding cybercrime (crimes connected with Internet use) has been drafted by the Council of Europe and, at the time of writing, has just been approved by the European Committee on Crimes Problems. It makes it a crime to:

1. Deal in child pornography
2. Reproduce or distribute copyright material without permission
3. Spread racist propaganda

Although the treaty will allow individual states to deal with cybercrime, it will set an international standard for Internet activities in the future.

The best way to protect children from such harmful material is by supervising their Internet activities, by placing the computer in a 'busy' area of the home, i.e. not tucked away in the attic, and by educating them as they use it. There are also some software packages, which can filter out material that is deemed unsuitable for children i.e. pornographic, violent or drug related material. Unfortunately, some of this software can be too restrictive and will censor potentially educational sites. For example, if a package filters out the word 'sex', then even sites which use the word to mean 'gender' will be inaccessible. Many of the packages have automatic upgrading facilities, checking new sites for sensitive material. This means, in effect, that someone else is deciding what to censor for you. Some search engines can provide a parental guard that will deny access to certain sites. If parents want to bypass the guard they just type in a password and it will be turned off. There are also a number of child-safe search engines, which contain a list of sites which are specifically aimed at children and young students, and many of which are educational and useful for researching homework assignments.

 # Internet Addiction

Internet Addiction Disorder is a new medical term that has been proposed for a condition in which users find they cannot live without a regular Internet 'fix'. The effects include relationships and marriages breaking up, regular absenteeism from work and forgetting to eat and sleep. The most common types are chat room, email, gambling and business addiction.

 # Digital Divide

The World Wide Web is actually a very misleading term. Of course we can communicate with Internet users from all corners of the globe, but at the time of writing it can be stated that over half the world's population has never used a telephone. The percentage of Internet users worldwide is in the region of 6% (*www.digitaldividenetwatch.org*) and there are more Internet users in New York City than in the whole of the African continent.

These can be startling figures, especially when many of us take these communication technologies for granted. Some argue that in order for the Third World to catch up with the West it needs access to this type of technology, which can help inform and educate people in areas such as food production and health care. However, others believe that they should first reach adequate levels of literacy and wealth before being supplied with computers. The digital divide doesn't just exist between developed nations and the Third World but also between the rich and poor within individual countries. There are concerns that if this divide is not bridged, it will lead to an even greater divide, and those who cannot afford the technology, will be left behind in a world that is becoming increasingly dependent on the Internet.

Digital Music

The digital music revolution has been causing quite a stir amongst fans, bands, artists and record companies. MP3 is a technology that allows music to be stored on a computer file. This tempted many individuals to put their entire CD collections onto MP3 files and share them with millions of others across the Internet. The most famous agent to provide this service was Napster, which was taken to court by record companies and some musicians, who believed it was damaging music sales and they were losing profits, since people were getting music for free over the Web. They said that it was breaking copyright laws by illegally distributing free music across the Internet without the musicians' or record companies' permission. Some companies, seeing the potential for profit, jumped on the bandwagon and started developing their own online music services. In July 2001, Napster was shut down by the US federal courts, but German record company Bertelsmann AG has done a deal with Napster to create a subscription service, which, at the time of writing, is still at the development stage.

Chapter Review

1. In what way is the Internet different from other forms of mass media?
2. Make a list of the main uses of the Internet?
3. What are the advantages and disadvantages of chat rooms?
4. What are the main security issues of Internet use?
5. What is the difference between the Internet and the World Wide Web?
6. Outline the main points of the Department of Justice report on illegal uses of the Internet.
7. What are the advantages and disadvantages of shopping online?
8. Outline the chief concerns of the Internet.

Assignment or Discussion Topics

'Everyone is equal on the Internet.'

'People are becoming too dependent on technology.'

'Technology isolates people from the real world of human emotion and contact. They are losing their social skills and the ability to communicate face-to-face.'

'The Internet gives people the confidence to communicate like they never could in the real world.'

Some useful websites:

Employment related sites:

www.monster.ie

www.irishjobs.ie

www.headhunt.ie

www.alljobz.com

www.workthing.com

www.jobsnation.net

Internet/technology related sites:

www.amarach.com

www.globalchange.com

www.learnthenet.com

www.nua.ie

www.wired.com

www.isc.ie

http://netculture.about.com/mbody.htm?once=true&

http://europa.eu.int/ISPO/legal/en/infolaw.html

http://www.qlinks.net/

http://libertus.net/liberty/debategl.html#Ireland

Chapter 22 Email

FETAC Assessment Requirements
Communication Technology Skills

Topics Covered

Netiquette

Business/Formal Email

Sending

Replying

Forwarding

Attachments

Address Book

Email at Work

THE e-MAIL OF THE SPECIES
IS MORE DEADLY THAN THE MAIL.

Fig. 22.1

Email, or electronic mail, is a way of sending messages via the Internet from one computer to another. It is has quickly become one of the most popular forms of distance communication, and is the most popular application of the Internet. In fact, it is revolutionising the way we communicate. We can send a message to anyone in the world who has an email address without worrying about handwriting, letterheads, printing, envelopes, stamps or going to the post office. If we want to communicate with someone who is asleep on the other side of the world, we can send them a message and have a reply when we get up the next morning. Another advantage is the storage space. It is possible to store all the emails we send and receive on a relatively small amount of disk space.

Nowadays people are as likely to exchange email addresses as telephone numbers. Email has obvious advantages over other forms of distance communication. It is cheaper than a phone call, faster than the postal service ('snail mail') and more efficient than a fax. This makes it very appealing and almost essential for any business.

The cost of sending an email is the cost of a phone call to your local Internet Service Provider, even if you are mailing someone at the other side of the world. As with phone calls, it is often cheaper to send mail in the evening or at weekends. It is also cheaper to read and write emails while offline and only send and receive them while online. Email is sent from the sender of the message via their ISP to the receiver's ISP where they are stored until the receiver logs on. Then the ISP will send any messages to the receiver's computer.

Most new computers come with an email package already installed. Internet Explorer includes the Outlook Express email package. However you also need to set up an account, which usually comes with the ISP registration.

Webmail is a free mail facility attached to a website. It is useful for when we are travelling because we can access it from any Web connected computer in the world. One disadvantage is that we must be online when using this facility, and therefore it is more expensive. Here are some of the most popular Webmail services:
- *www.hotmail.com*
- *www.mail.yahoo.com*
- *www.ireland.com*
- *www.oceanfree.net*
- *www.planetaccess.com*

Email is not a secure way of communicating. It is possible for someone to intercept it en route to its destination. It is like sending a postcard and therefore it is important to treat it as such. If someone knows our email password and the details of our ISP account they can access our messages, therefore we should never divulge our password to anyone.

Netiquette

One of the appeals of email is its speed and ease of use. However, this means we tend to write and send messages as casually as if we were speaking to someone. Like mobile text messages, email is a curious hybrid of spoken and written communication and the style is often chatty and informal. When starting out, people often find it takes them a while before they become really comfortable with it.

Due to its informality and conversational style, care needs to be taken when composing and sending messages. Words that are spoken have the advantage of tone and NVC to convey feelings in a message. We can say to a friend, 'Get lost' and they may sense the fun in our voice or in our facial expression. Words that are in cold print, however, have a different effect. They are not supported or modified by NVC and can seem a little less friendly. They also don't disappear as quickly as spoken words and linger before our eyes. What may seem trivial and fun to the sender, may be taken up the wrong way by the receiver. We should therefore re-read every email before sending.

One way of adding tone or expression to our emails is by using emoticons. Emoticons are symbols which combine various punctuation marks to indicate emotions. Here are some examples:

- :-)   smile
- :-D   laughter
- :-o   shock
- :-(frown
- :'-(crying
- ;-)   wink
- 0:-)   angel
- }:->   devil
- :8)   pig
- X-)   I see nothing
- :-X   I'll say nothing

Never type a message in capitals as this shows annoyance and is called shouting. Sending someone personal abuse is called flaming.

When we go online and access our email we check the *Inbox* where our new email is stored. The *Outbox* is where emails that are waiting to be sent are kept. The sent email box stores all emails we have sent and depending on what email package we have, there may be a *Deleted Items* box, for email removed from the *Inbox*, but not completely deleted. *Drafts* is for storing unfinished emails and saving them until later.

Business/Formal Email

The normal rules of letter writing do not apply to email. So how do we write a formal email, say as a business communication or as an application for a job? There are no fixed rules here, and very often the style is still informal and chatty. The sender's address and the date will automatically be sent with the mail and the sender writes the subject in the subject box (see below). However, whereas people seldom start an email with the traditional 'Dear Sir' or finish with 'Yours faithfully', we cannot begin a serious mail with 'Hi John'. The current standards are 'Dear' or 'Hello' followed by a name (Mr/Ms etc.), or just the name on its own, and the close is 'Regards' or 'Kind Regards' followed by the sender's full name. It may well happen that we receive a reply in a far more informal tone than in the mail we sent or expect, but it is better to err on the side of formality at the outset. Let the prospective employer or client set the tone thereafter. At present, you shouldn't apply for a job by email unless it has been specifically requested. Most employers today still require a handwritten letter.

 # Sending

Above the message box are a number of lines for addresses and the subject:

1. *To*: Write the recipient's address in here. It must be exactly right, otherwise it will be sent straight back. If you have contacts in your address book, then you need only type in their nickname as it appears in the address book, and it will be sent to them.
2. *Cc*: This line is for 'carbon copy' if you want to send the message to more than one person. Separate each address with a semi-colon.
3. *Bcc*: If you don't want the recipients to know who else is getting the mail, put their addresses in here. It stands for 'blind carbon copy'. However every recipient can see who is in the *To*: and *Cc*: box, so to send emails without anyone knowing any other recipient, put your own address in the *To*: line and the rest in Bcc:
4. *Subject*: Type in a subject keyword or phrase here to let the recipients know what the message is about. If you don't type in a subject, an error message will remind you and you have the option of sending it without one.

All email facilities enable us to add our own personal touch to our messages. A *Signature* file means we can add our address, phone number, or even a witty remark that will appear at the bottom of every email we send.

 # Replying

It is considered polite to reply to emails as promptly as possible. Since it is such a fast method of communicating, there should be no excuse. Even one line, acknowledging receipt of an email is enough. When replying, just click on *Reply* and a box with the original message opens and you can type your new message into it. The original message can be changed or deleted as required. It can be fun to reply to an email by creating an 'interview'. Leave extracts and any questions from the sender in the reply, and add responses below them. The sender's original quotes will be preceded by a chevron (>). After composing the new message, simply click on *Send*. The *Reply to All* option will send the message to everyone who received the original message, if there was more than one recipient.

Forwarding

Occasionally we receive messages that we'd like to send on to someone else. To forward a message, click on the *Forward* button, the message is copied into a new email and you simply fill in the name of the new recipient. Many humorous messages get passed around this way, and often travel right across the globe. Some individuals send nothing but forwards, much to the annoyance of their friends and contacts. A problem with forwards is that you might be exposing people's private email addresses to others without their consent.

Attachments

The attachment facility enables us to send pictures, word-processed documents, spreadsheets, scanned images, and even programs, in other words, we can attach any of these to an email we are sending. Lengthy documents can take a long time to send. As many computer viruses can be transmitted via attachments, never open an attachment from someone you do not trust or know. It could destroy hundreds if not all the files on your computer if it is affected. We know we have received an attachment when a paper clip appears beside the message in the Inbox. Always save an attachment to disk before opening. Then run a virus check on it and open it as a normal file.

To send an attachment, simply click on *Attachment* and from the window select and click the file you want to send. Click *Attach* and it will return you to your email with the file attached. Then send the email as normal.

Address Book

At first email addresses seem to be very long and difficult to remember, but when you get used to them they become easier to recall. As you collect addresses from friends and contacts and from emails you can store them in your address book. It is advisable to print out a hard copy of your addresses in case your computer crashes and the file is lost.

Email at Work

Many companies allow their employees to have free access to their Internet and email facilities. The speed and efficiency of the technology is an obvious benefit to business and many companies also have a LAN (Local Area Network) for sending and receiving internal messages. In recent years some companies have fired employees for sending offensive emails on the company's account, and for messages that could damage the company's reputation which in turn might result in financial loss. Many companies believe it is their right to monitor employees' email for a number of reasons. Firstly, the company pays the bills. Secondly, they feel it should be used primarily for business communications. Thirdly, there is the threat of computer viruses. At the time of writing there is no legislation in Ireland to prevent an employer monitoring employees' emails. Some would see this as an intrusion into privacy. The Data Protection Commissioner has suggested that it is up to the individual employer to let workers know that Internet and email use is done on the company's time and at their expense. Employees should also be informed if and how supervision will take place, and employers must minimise intrusion into workers' privacy. A climate of open and honest communication for all concerned usually helps in such situations.

Email is about the essence of written communication – words. This is what makes it so popular: short, swift messages that are straight to the point.

We should take care not to *spam*, that is sending large quantities of email which clog up someone's in box, or their entire system. Because it is so easy to send emails we may be tempted to overdo it, so exercising a little restraint is no bad thing.

Summary points:

1. Always re-read emails before sending
2. Always save attachments to disk and check before opening
3. Think about what information you send – it's as readable as a postcard
4. Avoid SHOUTING and flaming.

Assessment Activity

If the facilities are available, open a free email account at *www.hotmail.com* or *www.oceanfree.net* follow the registration instructions and send and receive at least one email. For beginners this might take one or even two class periods.

Discussion

1. What advantages and disadvantages have you experienced with email?
2. What suggestions and recommendations would you give to others using email?
3. What are the issues involved in sending forwards en masse to your contacts?

 # Chapter Review

1. What rules of netiquette apply to email?
2. What are the main issues regarding the use of email at work?

Chapter 23 Mass Communication

Mass communication consists of messages and meanings that are sent and received on a mass scale via what we call the mass media. Before the invention of the printing press, news and information was generally passed by word of mouth, letters or public notices. The first daily newspaper was founded in London in 1702. Newspapers reached mass circulation after the industrial revolution in the 1800s. The nineteenth and twentieth centuries have seen rapid advances in technologies, which have converged giving us today's Internet, television, newspapers, magazines, books, advertising, video, radio, cinema and popular music.

Mass communication differs from other forms of communication in a number of ways:
1. It is chiefly a one-way process – messages are transmitted from a 'producer' to an 'audience'. Messages can be sent back via letters to a newspaper editor, reviews of CDs, films, books etc. but their size and impact is tiny by comparison.
2. Its size – 'mass' means large whether it's cost, audience, production, number and size of messages.
3. Technologies – all forms of media use the latest technologies for creating, storing and reproducing their information.
4. It is an industry – its messages are products that are bought and sold.

Control of the Media

With something so widespread, powerful and influential in our lives we need to look behind the scenes and explore how it is controlled and by whom. If there are individuals who have sway over the media, whether we agree with them or not, we have a right to know who they are and if they have an agenda or set of values they might be trying to communicate. We could also ask if they are getting out of control. Many critics today view the enormous and rapid changes taking place in the media world as a serious cause of concern, as the media are becoming so powerful and influential that some governments have been suspected of bending to their wishes.

Ownership – Moguls and Mergers

In recent years a smaller number of major media companies has been acquiring ownership of a larger chunk of the media output. Media moguls are individuals who own or preside over large media companies. Perhaps the best known example is Rupert Murdoch, who owns a huge multimedia conglomerate called News Corporation. It publishes 175 different newspapers worldwide, it owns Fox Broadcasting, Twentieth Century Fox film studios, BskyB, Fox Sports Australia, STAR Television in Asia, National Geographic channel, various family and children's cable channels, HarperCollins book publishers, numerous magazines as well as the Los Angeles Dodgers Baseball team. In 1999, Murdoch lost a bid to buy Manchester United FC. This is only a small selection of what News Corp owns. For more information check the website at: *www.newscorp.com*

Independent News and Media, owned by Tony O'Reilly, is Ireland's largest media company. Amongst its publications are the *Irish Independent*, the *Sunday Independent*, the *Evening Herald* and the *Sunday World*. It also has a 50 per cent share in the *Star*, a 24.9 per cent share in the *Sunday Tribune* and various local newspapers which account for 40 per cent of the regional market. It owns a 50 per cent share in Princes Holdings Ltd., the second largest cable TV company in Ireland and publishes the Independent Telephone Directory. In 2000 it moved into the Internet sector, buying Internet Ireland, to provide Internet access to corporate clients, and formed a new company, Unison, a set top Internet connector. The group also has publications in the UK, Europe, Australia, South Africa, New Zealand and owns advertising in Mexico. Tony O'Reilly is also chairman of Heinz, one of the world's leading food companies.

Silvio Berlusconi owns three of Italy's most influential television channels, some of the country's largest construction and property companies, AC Milan football club and is the richest man in Italy. He is also thought to be one of the most corrupt politicians in Europe. Since the start of the 1990s he has been accused of bribery, perjury, falsification of financial documents, tax offences and collaboration with the Mafia. In four cases he was found guilty, but the sentences were lifted following appeals. In May 2001, he was elected Prime Minister of Italy for the second time.

Discussion

What does all this mean for the ordinary media consumer? Can we rely on the integrity of such powerful individuals? Will the information they provide be unbiased and truthful? Are their main concerns to do with providing quality information and entertainment or with making a profit and increasing their power? What do you know about their political affiliations?

In 2001, America Online (AOL), one of the largest Internet companies, merged with Time Warner, one of America's biggest media corporations. It was referred to at the time as the biggest deal in history. Gerald Levin, Chief Executive Officer (CEO) of Time Warner, said that such global media are becoming the predominant business of the twenty-first century, more important than government, more important than education and non-profits. Shortly after this, Time Warner merged with another media giant, EMI, thus creating the biggest record company in the world. What exists now is a marriage between the old media of the twentieth century –– news, cinema, popular music – and the new medium of the twenty-first century – the Internet. If more and more media will come to us via the Internet then AOL Time Warner is ideally positioned to reap the financial benefits.

When a small number of these media conglomerates own a large proportion of the media outlets, critics argue that they may have too much control over media output. The bigger they become the harder they are to control. What kind of news and entertainment will they provide? Will the news they deliver be objective? All the major media conglomerates share similar vested interests, which usually place corporate profit over other concerns such as the environment, workers and even the consumers. Such media concentration can prevent a healthy diversity of interests and viewpoints and minority interests might lose out.

Multimarketing is a modern media phenomenon that enables media giants to promote and sell their products across a range of their media outlets. For example, a book can be made into a film, reviewed in a newspaper, promoted by a soundtrack, released on video and sold to television all of which may belong to the one multimedia conglomerate. Then there is the merchandising. Toys, food and drink, clothes and accessories are all manufactured with the media brand attached to them. It is estimated that the *Star Wars* films may have earned in excess of $2 billion in merchandising alone. Commercial synergy is when two or more compatible media products are sold simultaneously, for example, *Trainspotting*, the film and its soundtrack.

Smaller, independent companies will find it harder to compete in such a world, and often the most innovative ideas come from these margins. Big business is concerned with more business and does not like to take risks so it will produce material that will guarantee profits. The heavy reliance of film companies on sequels is evidence of this. A sequel to a successful film is almost guaranteed to make a profit, so there is no financial risk, but often very little original creativity.

Activities

1. Amongst the largest media multinationals are: Viacom, Disney, AOL Time Warner, Warner EMI Music, News Corporation and Seagram. Find out, from the Internet if possible, what media outlets these companies own.
2. Research the multimarketing of a recent popular media product, identifying the media spin-offs such as music, books, videos etc.
3. We've seen who owns a number of the Irish newspapers. Find out who owns the following:
   (a) *The Irish Times*
   (b) *Examiner*
   (c) *Irish News*
   (d) *Sunday Business Post*
   (e) *Ireland on Sunday*
   (f) *Hot Press*
   (g) *Magill*
   (h) *Phoenix*

Regulation

Broadcasting

To balance out the vast private ownership of the media, government and independent regulation exerts a certain degree of control over media output. *Public Service Broadcasting* is the idea that the public should get what someone (e.g. the Government or a semi-state body) thinks it needs. RTÉ is a public service broadcaster, and as such its role is to provide information and entertainment to the public, which reflects the cultural diversity of Ireland and increases public understanding of the values and traditions of other countries. Education, art and culture, children's programmes, news, current affairs, documentaries and programmes with minority group interests as well as entertainment are all seen as part of that service. The RTÉ Authority is a nine-member committee appointed by the Government to supervise the running of the station and programme content, and in this way it is state regulated.

The Broadcasting Bill 2001 set up the Broadcasting Commission of Ireland, which is laying down a code of standards for Irish radio, television, and advertising. Under the new legislation, emphasis is still put on importance of public service broadcasting, but many media critics question whether this is relevant anymore.

In 2001, RTÉ wanted to increase its license fee by €63.50 (IR£50) so that it could cope with the huge increase in competition from commercial channels and to help in the transition to digital broadcasting. The Minister for Arts Culture and the Gaeltacht, Síle de Valera, capped the increase at €18.41 (IR£14.50) causing much controversy. RTÉ claims it cannot provide proper public service broadcasting with such little funding. Critics argue that RTÉ doesn't provide quality Irish programming, and instead relies on foreign-produced programmes and cheap re-runs. Some believe that the public doesn't want serious 'sensible' programmes provided by public service broadcasting, preferring to watch more entertaining material like sports, films, soap operas and quiz shows. Perhaps a more pertinent question is, how can the Government control broadcasting if most of it originates in other countries?

Discussion

Digital technology is completely transforming television. It offers more channels, better picture and sound quality, more interactivity, pay per view, Internet access, video on demand, improved teletext and more specialised channels. What are the advantages and disadvantages of this?

Commercial television and radio depends primarily on advertising, and therefore must convince advertisers that people are watching and listening. TV3 is controlled by an international media company, CanWest. To ensure that profits are made, costs are often kept down and programmes with as wide an appeal as possible are shown. Soaps and sitcoms are relatively cheap, as are repeats and medium quality films. However, commercial TV and radio don't have a commitment to educational or informative broadcasting as RTÉ does. This is fine as it means there is plenty of choice. However, in the new digital era when hundreds of commercial channels are competing for viewers, what sort of information and entertainment can we expect?

Activity

Do a brief survey in your class group to see what types of programmes are popular and which channels people watch the most. Is there a predominance of PBS or commercial television?

Censorship

Censorship occurs in the media when material is considered to be in some way offensive, obscene or a threat to security. Censorship laws vary from country to country, and some individuals believe that there should be no censorship whatsoever. Under the Constitution we all have freedom of expression, but that freedom is also restricted under a number of laws.

Film and Video Censorship

In Ireland the Office of the Film Censor is an associate office of the Department of Justice. The censor would generally question film material that is considered to be 'subversive of public morality' or blasphemous (The Censorship of Films Acts, 1923–92), but would also be guided by public opinion. Language, sex and violence are also determining factors.

The censor's main task is the classification of films, (general, PG, over 12, over 15 and over 18) which is to protect young people from viewing material that may shock or cause them harm. This poses the usual question: Do films (especially violent films) influence the way people behave? Studies have shown that most people are unaffected by such films. However, young people who are particularly vulnerable, who don't have adequate moral guidance or emotional support from parents or guardians and who have low intellectual skills can confuse reality with fiction, and may act out the behaviour they witness on a television or cinema screen.

Discussion

Films are rarely banned outright in Ireland, a notable exception being *Natural Born Killers* which was banned in 1995, due to its gratuitous violence (violence just for the sake of it). The film is now available on video. A number of murders in the US were linked to the film. In 1999, the ban on Stanley Kubrick's *A Clockwork Orange* was lifted after twenty-six years. At the time of its release it spawned copycat killings in Britain. *Monty Python's Life of Brian* was also banned for seven years after its initial release. Do you think these films should have been banned?

The Video Recordings Act 1989, provides that the censor may declare that a video is unfit for viewing if:

1. 'the viewing of it would be likely to cause persons to commit crimes...
2. 'the viewing of it would be likely to stir up hatred against a group...on account of their race, colour, nationality, religion, ethnic or national origins, membership of the travelling community or sexual orientation...
3. 'the viewing of it would tend, by reason of...obscene or indecent matter, to deprave or corrupt persons...
4. 'it depicts acts of gross violence or cruelty (including mutilation and torture) towards humans or animals'

Discussion

Do you think these are useful restrictions? Do you think they are necessary? How strictly are they applied? Who is ultimately responsible for safeguarding children with regard to videos? Find out how many in your class group have watched a video that was classified for an age they hadn't reached yet. How did they get the video?

Censorship of Publications

The Censorship of Publication Board banned *In Dublin* magazine in the summer of 1999 because it was allegedly 'indecent or obscene'. The Censorship of Publications Act 1929 (amended 1946, 1967) defines indecent as being 'suggestive of, or inciting to, sexual immorality or unnatural vice or likely in any other way to corrupt or deprave'. The likely reason for the ban was that the magazine had been advertising 'massage parlours' and 'health studios', which were most probably brothels, and therefore, illegal. Some commented that it was hardly material that could be called obscene. *Playboy* was banned for years, but the ban was lifted, not because it became less obscene, but because of a change in social standards.

Discussion

Do you think *In Dublin* should have been banned? How does it compare to magazines like *Playboy*?

Other Legislation

1. The Official Secrets Act 1963, amended 2000, states that it is illegal to communicate official information, which relates to defence, security, Northern Ireland and personal safety matters.
2. Under the Freedom of Information Act 1998, members of the public have a legal right to official information held by public bodies and Government departments unless it is connected with national security, defence, international relations or relating to Northern Ireland in accordance with the Official Secrets Act.

3. The Defamation Act 1961 – often referred to as the libel laws – prohibits the publishing or broadcasting of false information, which might harm a person's reputation, cause them to be hated or ridiculed, shunned or avoided by right-thinking members of society. Under the law, a person who believes they have been libelled, can take the journalist, publication or broadcaster to court and sue for damages. The costs can be enormous. Occasionally charges are dropped if the publication or broadcaster can prove the information is in the public interest, in other words that it is exposing corruption or criminal activity, or giving information that is in the interest of health or security, which the public has a right to know about.

Many journalists are critical of this legislation as they feel it restricts their ability to carry out investigative work and that it is contrary to freedom of expression and the Freedom of Information Act. The European Court of Human Rights has stated that the media has a right and a duty to keep the public informed, and to act as society's watchdog. As such it is seen as a vital part of the democratic system. Some maintain that former Taoiseach, Charles Haughey, escaped detection in the 1980s due to the strict libel laws. Of course others believe that someone should be watching the media since they are becoming so huge and uncontrollable.

In the light of the changes that the media are undergoing, amendments to the Defamation Act are being considered by the Government as part of a new legislative programme. Details may be found at the Government's website: *www.irlgov.ie*

Activity

Sometimes the public's right to know is contrary to the individual's right to privacy. To what degree is a person's private life a legitimate matter of public interest? Which of the following situations do you think are a legitimate matter of public interest, and should they be published:

1. A politician is revealed to be gay.
2. A member of the public contracts AIDS.
3. A politician's son is suspended from school for an incident involving drink. He is under age.
4. A paedophile is released from prison and goes to live in a housing estate inhabited by young families.
5. A famous pop star is found to be addicted to heroin.
6. An ordinary member of the public is involved in a workplace prank in which a new colleague is stripped and tied to a lamppost causing severe distress.
7. A politician has an extra marital affair.
8. A film star is seen nude sunbathing on a yacht.
9. A farmer owns a cow suspected of having BSE.
10. Two cabinet ministers, one, the Minister of Finance, the other the Tánaiste, take a holiday in the French villa of a major businessman.
11. A television presenter checks into a detox clinic.

Self Regulation

Apart from laws written into the Constitution, many media have their own self-regulatory bodies. Two examples are:

1. The Advertising Standards Authority of Ireland is a forum where complaints about advertisements, which are felt to be offensive or indecent, may be lodged.
2. The National Union of Journalists' Code of Conduct provides journalists and editors with guidelines on what they may or may not publish.

 # Advertising

An old saying goes: 'He who pays the piper calls the tune.' Advertising is persuasive communication that lies at the core of most media forms, so much so that it is considered a mass medium itself. Most forms of media are dependent on at least some advertising to survive.

Does advertising influence or control media output? An example of this occurred in 2000 when the *Sunday Independent* published an article which made offensive remarks about disabled people competing in the Paralympics. As a result of this, a group of 31 voluntary organisations, which called itself 'potential advertisers with Independent Newspapers', refused to advertise in the *Sunday Independent*. So here we see the advertisers exerting an influence, albeit a positive one, on the content of a newspaper. It could also work the other way around. Editors and producers, who may be dependent on advertisers for revenue, need to be sure they don't offend people who are a source of revenue.

The media have to sell space to advertisers to make revenue. Before a company will advertise they must first be convinced that there is an audience for their advertising. To be guaranteed an audience, the media have to provide something new, fresh and stimulating. Therefore, the media, with ever increasing competition, is under pressure to provide ever fresher, newer and more stimulating entertainment and information. This, commentators say, may reduce the amount of quality media available, as there is more and more reliance on shock tactics to win over audiences.

> ## Discussion
> 'Pester power' is a term that describes advertisers' targeting of young children in the hope that they will pester their parents into buying them certain products. It is particularly evident in the months leading up to Christmas. What do you think of this type of advertising? Have you ever seen pester power at work?

 # Audience

Readers, viewers and listeners, or more simply consumers, of the media are referred to in media studies as the 'audience'. To what extent does an audience have control over media output? Is the audience a group of dumb receivers, gobbling up whatever is put before them, or is it a collection of discerning discriminating individuals who make informed choices about what is good and bad? Audience tastes and preferences are constantly being checked and monitored by market researchers as they are the lifeblood of any media product. Not only do they provide revenue for the media through sales of tickets, licence fees, cover prices and so forth, but audiences, once targeted can be sold to the advertisers who can further target them with commercials that specifically cater to their tastes.

Activity

Look at the different types of advertisements in a variety of magazines and newspapers, or at different times of the day on television. This often indicates the type of audience at which the product is aimed.

Discussion

What kind of audience would the following appeal to and why:
- Westlife
- *The Sunday Business Post*
- Coronation Street
- Star Trek
- *Cosmopolitan*
- Match of the Day
- Toy Story
- Questions and Answers

Media audiences are active in their choice of what they want to read, view and hear. However, an audience must also depend upon whatever is available. Media analysts often complain that today the media are dumbing down, aiming for the lowest common denominator because that is what will sell. They maintain the audience is only important to media producers in terms of the numbers they can sell to advertisers and not whether the material has any real quality.

Discussion

Debates rage about the definition of the word 'quality', and whether the media should provide what the public wants or what the public needs. What does quality mean to you? What is quality in terms of the following, and why:
- News
- Cinema
- Television
- Radio
- Books
- Magazines
- Popular Music

Opinions naturally will vary, but is there a standard and who sets it? Should we be told what is good for us, in the way public service broadcasting does, or should we be allowed to decide for ourselves?

Selection and Production

It can be interesting to ask why a television programme uses such and such a camera shot or angle, or soundtrack, or actor, or why a newspaper uses a particular news story as its headline, or photograph to accompany it. All these considerations are a result of a selection process carried out by a team of media personnel each contributing their ideas and input, shaping and reshaping the raw material to create a completed media commodity.

In recent years 'real' television has proved to be a highly successful format. Channel 4's *Big Brother* and all the other European versions claimed to show real people in real situations. But how real *was* it and how much of it was mediated and constructed? It is well to consider that

Fig. 23.1 Republican Militiaman.

information that is left out of the picture is sometimes as important as that which is left in. A photograph in a newspaper may be cropped to show only a segment of what was really happening. Film directors ask actors to do numerous 'takes' in order to get a scene exactly the way they want it.

When this picture was originally published in *The Irish Times*, the mouth was omitted. Why do you think this was done? What difference would it make?

The information that has been omitted might reveal a different truth. A news item might be selected simply because it has accompanying dramatic images. The media only show us a representation of reality, even though they may sometimes try to convince us otherwise. *Gatekeepers* are the people who decide along the way what gets added or omitted during the process of mediation. They might have any number of reasons for allowing material through the 'gates', based upon their own personal taste, their political persuasions, religious beliefs, the demands of the market or the fear of legal proceedings.

Look at these two photographs taken in Genoa during the G8 summit in July 2001. Since only a small minority of the protesters were involved in violence, why do you think these two photographs were selected? What is the initial impression a reader might get of the protests? Is this accurate photojournalism?

Figure 23.2 Anti-globalisation protests.

Tabloidisation

The word 'tabloid' originally referred to newspapers which were printed on A3 sized paper. It gradually took on the connotation of brashness and sleaze because the news in such papers was considered to be sensational, titillating and sometimes dirty. Murders, scandal and human-interest stories were reported in an easy-to-read, entertaining format.

In the 1970s Rupert Murdoch introduced the 'page three girl' to *The Sun* resulting in a substantial sales increase. In the 1980s he introduced a bingo game and cut the price ensuring the paper would become a runaway success. In that decade, Lady Diana Spencer became Princess Di, the most photographed woman in the world, appearing regularly on the front covers of tabloid newspapers. Some people, including her brother, Earl Spencer, blamed the tabloid press for her death, because the car in which she was travelling when it crashed, was speeding to escape the attention of press photographers. Tabloid editors would argue that they merely publish what the public wants.

Tabloids are often accused of being responsible for the dumbing down of the media. Perhaps this is a result of the language used by them. Studies have shown that the language used in tabloid newspapers is simple enough for a six-year-old to understand. The style of language in a tabloid is quite different to that of the broadsheets. It is usually dramatic, witty, emotive, crude and sometimes violent. It makes use of the first person ('We believe...') and is often highly subjective. Broadsheets try to avoid such a style as it is believed that it shows bias.

Discussion

Should news be infotainment (information that is entertaining) or purely information? Newspaper editors know that shock and sensation sells. Some observers say it is now occurring in television and tabloid TV is a style of sensationalist television that uses the techniques of the tabloid newspapers. When TV3 was set up, it aimed to produce news that was bright and breezy. Its weather forecasters play requests. Is this excessively entertaining?

Think of examples of television shows that use shock and sensation tactics to attract audiences. What is the appeal in them? How many in the class group watch them regularly?

 # Media Values – Not Just Entertainment

A society's values are determined by its main institutions such as the Government, the courts, religious and educational organisations and the media. The media send out messages about what we accept as being normal in our culture, giving them enormous power and influence. They both reflect and are influenced by society's cultural norms and values, and people and events are represented in such a way that they fit into our assumptions about them.

The values and ideology of society are seldom questioned in mainstream media, especially the entertainment industry. Since so much of the media is now produced by large multi-national corporations, it is likely that most of the values portrayed by the media will be influenced by the interests of big business. Challenging stereotypes and questioning society's values are themes that are more often found in independently produced and peripheral media, and the more the multi-media conglomerates control the output, the less diverse the range of opinions on important issues. There is always the possibility that not all sections of society, e.g. minority groups and interests, will receive equal representation within the media. If, as it has been said, the media are becoming more important and often more powerful than governments, we might ask, who is really in control, and how will they help shape future societies?

Fig. 23.3 Kellogg's Special K ad.

What values are being communicated by this Kellogg's Special K ad? What are the connotations?

Discussion

1. Look at other advertisements from newspapers and magazines, or recall television, radio or cinema ads. How are the people in them represented? Do they contain any subtle connotations? Do they promote any particular cultural values?
2. *The Irish Times* recently created the position of Racial and Social Affairs correspondent. What does this tell us about contemporary Irish culture? What does this tell us about *The Irish Times*?

Activity

Metro Éireann is an Irish multi-cultural free sheet. What do you know about it? Find out where it is produced and by whom.

1. When was the last time you came across a media text that questioned your values and the way you live? If we accept the values of the mainstream media, who ultimately benefits?
2. When was the last time you encountered members of a minority group in the media? How were they portrayed? What was the setting?
3. What views and interests do you have that are not part of mainstream media which you would like to see more of?
4. In Ireland a number of celebrity magazines have recently arrived on our newsagent shelves such as *VIP* and *Who*. What does this tell us about our changing cultural values? Why have these magazines emerged in the last number of years?

Further Activities/Assignment Topics

1. Carry out research on a media mogul or a large multi-media conglomerate. Look at the history, current status and ownership and explore some opinions of media commentators.
2. What are the affects of the media on children? Pay particular attention to advertising, television, video and violence.
3. Censorship – is it necessary and is it relevant in today's global media climate?
4. Media intrusion – freedom of the press or an invasion of privacy?
5. Research the emergence in the 1980s and the current state of the Irish Film Industry.
6. Many companies that produce sports and leisure clothing have been accused of operating 'sweatshops', i.e. clothing factories with poor working conditions, in South-east Asia. Find out information on any of the following companies: GAP, Nike, Reebok, Addidas regarding their manufacturing policies and conditions.
7. Find out the latest circulation figures of Irish newspapers and magazines and the latest television ratings.

Chapter Review

1. What is public service broadcasting?
2. What is meant by self-regulation?
3. What is the purpose of censorship? Outline Ireland's current censorship laws.
4. Give a brief explanation of the Freedom of Information Act.
5. Give a brief explanation of the Defamation Act. Why is it unpopular with the press?
6. How could advertising influence media output?
7. Explain the significance of the audience in the media.
8. Give a brief explanation of the following:

(a) mogul

(b) merger

(c) multimarketing

(d) the public interest

(e) tabloidisation

(f) dumbing down

(g) lowest common denominator

(h) media selection

(i) pester power

(j) gatekeeper.

Appendix 2

FETAC assessment requirements and relevant chapters at a glance.

FETAC Assessment	Chapter(s)
Oral Presentation	10, 11, 12, 13, 14, **18**
Dialogue	10, 12, 13, 14, **15**, **16**, **19**
Discussion and Negotiation	10, 12, 13, 14, **15**, **17**
Message Taking/Giving	13, 14, **19**
Visual Communication Skills	**11**
Assignment	**7**, **8**
Personal and Business Documentation	**4**, **5**, **6**, **17**
Communication Technology Skills	**19**, 20, **21**, **22**

Bibliography

Agostini, Franco, *Visual Games*, London: Macdonald & Co. 1988.

Barry, Anne Marie Seward, *Visual Intelligence. Perception, Image and Manipulation in Visual Communication*, Albany: State University of New York 1997.

BBC Online, *Science. The Human Face*, 2001 [Online] *http://www.bbc.co.uk/science/humanbody/humanface/exp_relating.shtml* 13 June 2001.

Beddows, Christopher, *Communication Pack*, Maidenhead, Berks: McGraw-Hill 1991.

Bryson, Bill, *Mother Tongue: the English Language*, London: Penguin 1990.

Butler, Richard, *The Internet Demystified*, Dublin: Oak Tree Press 2000.

The Complete Letter Writer, Foulsham: Berkshire 1998.

Cairncross, Frances, *The Death of Distance. How the Communications Revolution will change our lives*, London: Orion Business 1997.

Chalker, Sylvia, and Edmund Weiner, *The Oxford Dictionary of English Grammar*, Oxford: Oxford University Press 1994.

Coffey, J. 'Nelson Mandela in Trinity' *Trinity Today*, Issue 6, (2000/2001) 17.

Cohen, Marlene C., Hawkins, Tony, Richardson, Susie, *Speech Communication. Multicultural Activities for the Group Communication Classroom*, [Online], *http://college.hmco.com/communication/speech/multigrp.htm#intro*, June 2001.

Council of Europe Press Service, *Council of Europe's Committee on Crime Problems approves final draft of Cyber-crime Convention*, 2001 [Online], *http://press.coe.int/cp/2001/456a(2001).htm*, July 2001.

Daunt, Stephen, *Communication Skills*, Dublin: Gill & Macmillan 1996.

Department of Justice, Equality and Law Reform, *Illegal and Harmful Use of the Internet. First Report of the Working Group*, Dublin: The Stationery Office 1997.

Dimbleby, Richard, and Graeme Burton, *More Than Words. An Introduction to Communication*, London: Routledge 1992.

Donohoe, Josephine, and Frances Gaynor, *Education and Care in the Early Years. A Textbook for Irish Students*, Dublin: Gill & Macmillan 1999.

EurekAlert, *Genetically Speaking, Race Doesn't Exist in Humans*, 1998 [Online], *http://www.eurekalert.org/pub_releases/1998-10/WUiS-GSRD-071098.php*, June 2001.

Floyd, G., McKay, J., *Writing a Bibliography (Harvard System)*, 2001 [Online], *http://www.dicksonc.act.edu.au/Library/bibliog.html*, 15 July 2001.

Forsyth, Patrick, *30 Minutes before a presentation*, London: Kogan Page 1997.

Foy, Geoffrey, *Text Production with Microsoft Word*, Dublin: Gill and Macmillan 2001.

General Assembly of the United Nations, *Universal Declaration of Human Rights*, [Online], *http://www.un.org/Overview/rights.html*, 26 July 2001.

Goff, Linda, *Ireland. 2000 World Press Freedom Review*, 2000 [Online], *http://www.freemedia.at/wpfr/ireland.htm*, June 2001.

Greenwald, Barry, *The Art of Communication*, [Online], *http://www.uic.edu/orgs/convening/communic.htm*, June 2001.

Horgan, John, *Irish Media. A Critical History Since 1922*, London: Routledge 2001.

Hurst, Bernice, *The Handbook of Communication Skills*, London: Kogan Page 1996.

Janner, Greville, *Janner's Complete Letter Writer*, London: Business Books Ltd. 1983.

Kennedy, Angus J., *The Rough Guide to the Internet*, London: Rough Guides Ltd. 2000.

Lester, Paul Martin, *Visual Communication: Images with Messages*, Belmont, California: Wadsworth/Thomson Learning 2000.

McClave, Henry, *Communication for Business*, Dublin: Gill & Macmillan 1997.

McCroskey, James C., *An Introduction to Rhetorical Communication*, Massachusetts: Allyn and Bacon 2001.

Mandel, Steve, *Effective Presentation Skills*, London: Kogan Page 1987.

Microsoft Encarta '98 Encyclopedia, Microsoft Corporation 1993-1997.

Morgan, John, and Peter Welton, *See What I Mean. An Introduction to Visual Communication*, London: Edward Arnold 1986.

Morris, Desmond, *Manwatching*, London: Triad 1978.

Pemberton, Lyn, and Simon Shurville, *Words on the Web*, Exeter: Intellect Books 2000.

Pinker, Stephen, *The Language Instinct*, London: Penguin Books 1994.

Public Communications Centre, *Citizen Traveller*, 1999 [Online], *http://www.pcc.ie/project/ctrav.html*, June 2001.

Purves, Bryan, *Information Graphics*, Cheltenham: Stanley Thornes 1987.

Putnam, Robert D., *Bowling Alone: America's Declining Social Capital*, 1995 [Online], *http://muse.jhu.edu/demo/journal_of_democracy/v006/putnam.html*, June 2001.

Quinlan, Ronan (Ed.) *National Union of Journalists, Dublin Branch* [Online] *http://indigo.ie/~nujdub/*, 26 July 2001.

Raha, Maria, *Angel*, 1999 [Online], *http://www.storybytes.com/view-stories/2000/angel.html*, July 2001.

Rivers, Denis, *Cooperative Communication Skills Workbook & Reader* 2001 [Online], *http://www.coopcomm.org/w7chal2.htm*, 25 July 2001.

Scher, Anna, and Charles Verrall, *100 + Ideas for Drama*, Oxford: Heinemann Educational 1975.

Scott, John F., *English Communications for Business Studies*, Dublin: Gill & Macmillan 2000.

Seely, John, *Dramakit*, Oxford: Oxford University Press 1977.

Solomon, Norman, *AOL Time Warner: Calling the Faithful to their Knees* [Online], *http://www.fair.org/media-beat/000113.html*, 26 July 2001.

Stanton, Nicky, *Mastering Communication*, London: Macmillan 1990.

Swann, Alan, *Communicating with Rough Visuals*, Oxford: Phaidon Press 1989.

Weiner, E. S. C., and Andrew Delahunty, *The Oxford Guide to English Usage*, Oxford: Oxford University Press 1994.

Winser, Jill (Ed.), *Future Talk. BT, Millennium Project. A Special Millennium Initiative*, London: Forward Publishing 2000.

Wood, Julia T., *Communication in our Lives*, Stamford, CT: Wadsworth, Thomson Learning 2000.